Luminos is the Open Access monograph publishing program
from UC Press. Luminos provides a framework for preserving and
reinvigorating monograph publishing for the future and increases
the reach and visibility of important scholarly work. Titles published
in the UC Press Luminos model are published with the same high
standards for selection, peer review, production, and marketing as
those in our traditional program. www.luminosoa.org

Higher Powers

Higher Powers

Alcohol and After in Uganda's Capital City

———

China Scherz, George Mpanga,
and Sarah Namirembe

中

UNIVERSITY OF CALIFORNIA PRESS

University of California Press
Oakland, California

Suggested citation: Scherz, C., Mpanga, G. and Namirembe, S. *Higher Powers: Alcohol and After in Uganda's Capital City*. Oakland: University of California Press, 2024. DOI: https://doi.org/10.1525/luminos.176

Library of Congress Cataloging-in-Publication Data

Names: Scherz, China, author. | Mpanga, George (Social scientist), author. | Namirembe, Sarah, 1988–author.
Title: Higher powers : alcohol and after in Uganda's capital city / China Scherz, George Mpanga, and Sarah Namirembe.
Description: Oakland, California : University of California Press, [2024] | Includes bibliographical references and index.
Identifiers: LCCN 2023022681 | ISBN 9780520396791 (paperback) | ISBN 9780520396807 (ebook)
Subjects: LCSH: Alcoholism—Uganda—Kampala. | Recovering alcoholics—Uganda—Kampala. | Alcoholics—Rehabilitation—Uganda—Kampala. | Alternative medicine—Uganda—Kampala.
Classification: LCC HV5283.U332 K367 2024 | DDC 362.292096761—dc23/eng/20230828

LC record available at https://lccn.loc.gov/2023022681

32 31 30 29 28 27 26 25 24 23
10 9 8 7 6 5 4 3 2 1

Ekitabo kino tukiwaayo eri abali mu kusoomozebwa, era tuli wamu nabo.

We dedicate this book to all people who have struggled or are still struggling.
We are in this together.

CONTENTS

ACKNOWLEDGMENTS

Writing this book has been a truly collaborative effort, as our work transformed and took shape through conversations in bars, herbal medicine shops, seminar rooms, rehabilitation centers, churches, Zoom workshops, conference panels, shrines, traffic jams, forests, coffeeshops, and living rooms.

Our deepest thanks go to the people who you will meet in the following pages, especially those who so generously shared their experiences with alcohol with us and who welcomed us into the lives that they have created beyond it. We also extend profound thanks to the healers who taught us about herbal medicine, rehabilitation, Alcoholics Anonymous, Pentecostal and Charismatic healing, and mediumship. We must also give a special word of appreciation to Dr. David Basangwa at Butabika Hospital. Through his enthusiasm, curiosity, and commitment to his patients Dr. Basangwa encouraged us to look beyond the clinic and also provided us with tremendous insight and practical advice along the way.

We also want to thank Noah Wabwire, Valentine Mujuzi, and Sebulime Hope Francis for the countless hours they spent driving us through Kampala traffic jams and beyond and for all of the invaluable insights they shared with us as we talked along the way.

We also want to thank the undergraduate researchers who contributed their time and talents to the project over the course of the past ten years. Among these students are Karina Atkins, Christy Audeh, Aubrey Bauer, Beza Bogale, Likita Griffith, Claire Mooney, Noorjahan Sheikh, Morgan Suchin, Emily Weisenberger, and Priscilla Opoku Yeboah. Amber Colby and Anne Nelson Stoner deserve special recognition here for the tremendous contributions they made to the project during the time they spent in Uganda with us.

A wide network of fellow scholars has also contributed to this work through their participation in numerous workshops, conferences, and conversations. Among those who shared their insights and friendship with us are: Vincanne Adams, Eniola Afolayan, Anne Alison, Cory-Alice Andre-Johnson, Ira Bashkow, Joshua Burraway, Jennifer Cole, Mackenzie Cramblit, Nomi Dave, Joseph Davis, Rebecca Dillingham, Jonathan Earle, Anna Eisenstein, Omri Elisha, Tess Farmer, Aidan Seale Feldman, Mayanthi Fernando, Gertrude Fraser, Brian Goldstone, Courtney Handman, Helena Hansen, Peter Hoesing, Jim Igoe, Erin Jordan, Jaideep Kapur, Fred Klaits, Stacey Langwick, Adria LaViolette, Julie Livingston, Abby Mack, David Kaawa Mafigiri, Samuel Maling, Cheryl Mattingly, Susan McKinnon, Louise Meintjes, George Mentore, Larry Merkel, Marissa Mika, Amira Mittermaier, Erin Moore, Robert Orsi, Kwame Edwin Otu, Ray Qu, Joel Robbins, Charles Rwabukwali, Peter Redfield, Godfrey Zari Rukundo, Harris Solomon, Scott Stonington, Sylvia Tidey, Rachel Wahl, Kath Weston, Jarrett Zigon, and Tyler Zoanni. We also thank our editor Kate Marshall, our editorial associate Chad Attenborough, our copyeditor Catherine Osborne, and our three reviewers for the insights and encouragement they shared as they helped to bring this book to completion.

We thank the National Science Foundation (Award no. BCS-1758472), the University of Virginia, and the Mellon Foundation for providing us with the financial support necessary to carry out the research that informs this book. We also thank the University of Virginia's Institutional Review Board, Makerere University's Social and Behavioral Sciences Research Ethics Committee, and the Uganda National Council for Science and Technology for their guidance and approval of our protocols.

China thanks her sister Summer and her father Charlie for their encouragement. She thanks her two children, Iggy and Lucy, for their joyful embrace of their time in Uganda and their willingness to endure her time away from them. Most of all she wants to thank her husband, Paul Scherz, for the boundless practical, personal, and intellectual contributions he has made to this project.

George wishes to thank his wife Agnes for her support during our lengthy periods of work, sometimes away from home. He also thanks his children, especially Georgia who despite her young age showed interest in the writing; his brother Eric for encouragement and advice; and his mother Cecilia for her support to him and the team. Lastly, he thanks his father, the late Eric Lutwama, for teaching his children the value of learning Luganda deeply, which helped him to do his part in this project.

Sarah wishes to thank Christine, Deborah, her sister Damalie, her mother Damalie, and her brothers Ivan and Allan for the support rendered during this time.

Introduction

In August 2015, George went to meet a man named Kajumba[1] at his home, just off the Entebbe Road highway. Pastor Andrew had recommended that we meet him to learn something about the people who had stopped drinking through their involvement at his church, the Christian Glory Center, a large Pentecostal church near Kajumba's home. George had already tried to visit Kajumba three times at the church, but beyond a first introductory visit with Pastor Andrew, Kajumba had not yet kept an appointment. Now George was to meet him at his home. "You can't miss their house, it's the old one, from the 1960s," Pastor Andrew had instructed him. George had in fact seen that old house many times as he passed on this road, not knowing that it was Kajumba's. The house was a big one, and it was surrounded by a very large compound and shaded by palm and *mutuba* trees.

A girl collecting water at the family water tank directed George to the back of the compound, and George continued past the house down to the swampy area behind it. George had briefly met Kajumba only once before, and at first did not recognize his face. But when Kajumba stood up, his unusual height made him unmistakable. He was standing in front of one of the three rooms of the back boys' quarters, holding a hoe in his hands, a tin of bean seeds at his feet. His loose gray trousers were folded to the knee, and he was barefoot. Clearly wanting to get back to his planting, he asked George how long the interview would take. "I can only give you ten minutes today. I want those seeds to spend the night in this soil," he said, ushering George into his house.

In the first room there was a sofa set and George tried to sit down, but Kajumba passed through, calling George to continue to the next room. The other room had sofas too, but these looked newer. There was also an old computer monitor and keyboard, but no CPU. On the wall were pictures of Jesus and a placard reading "Jesus is the head of this family." Hanging on the wall there was also a portrait of an old man of about sixty and framed photos of a formal *kwanjula* ceremony and wedding. The groom in both was Kajumba. After the formalities of greetings and consent forms, Kajumba began to tell his story.

"I am fifty-three years old. I come from the line of Ssekabaka Tembo," he started. "I don't know when my father settled here, but he originally came from Buddu. My father was Catholic and wanted me to become a priest, but he took me out of seminary because of my poor grades. After attending a different secondary school, I came back to the family home and got a job nearby at a garment factory. I was earning well, but then Idi Amin was overthrown, the company was looted, and I lost my job. After that, I started slowly to taste *waragi*, and it gradually developed into a habit. My mother had connected me to a job in a restaurant, right next to [the] Peacock Bar. I was working but also seriously drinking alcohol, feeling like a youth. I was always with a group, most of them are dead now. I usually left work at the restaurant at 8:00 p.m., sometimes later than that. Remember, I told you that opposite the restaurant was the Peacock Bar. What followed is obvious. But I was clean and knew how to make money. I woke up very early and worked. I took five years, seven years, ten years—drinking in a respectable way. But when I clocked twelve years, alcohol said, 'You are now ours!' And I began doubling the amount that I took.

"I began to be a *lujuuju*, someone people knew as a serious drinker. But I still had money. I was a good brickmaker and the money I made from the bricks I invested in tomatoes. We have a lot of water here, so I created an irrigation system so that I could harvest tomatoes in the dry season. I remember one time I had a big harvest, and I was the only one in the area who had tomatoes, but because I had started taking alcohol stupidly and there were no phones then, the buyers looked for me in bars.

"This was in the late 1980s and our main drinking spot was under an avocado tree, where you have seen a new factory being built. We had a group called *Basajjabatudde* (the men are seated). There was one in our group who worked in a cooperative society as a chief accountant. He was later fired because of his drinking. But at that time, he used to come with money and buy for the whole group which had about twenty members. Whether or not you had money, he bought for you. We had a ten-liter bottle which we would fill with waragi and place in the center of the table. Each could take as much as he wanted, and it would be refilled by that man many times.

"Over time, alcohol built a house on me, and I gradually failed to cultivate food. By the time of the first morning call to prayer at the mosque, I was already holding a *lubanto* bottle (250ml) of waragi in my hands. For a time that bottle could allow me to work, but over time I couldn't even raise up my head. Alcohol weakened my legs. I lost my appetite. And I totally stopped working.

"To get money to drink, I started selling things from the house. I was unmarried and living in the boys' quarters. Before I started drinking seriously, I used to select nice clothes, but eventually I sold all my clothes. I used to pray for sunshine so that I could wash and quickly dry the only shirt and trousers I had left. Then

I sold the beds, the cups. Eventually, even my fellow drinkers chased me away from their group because I stopped bathing and washing my clothes. By this stage, I couldn't bathe. When I tried to bathe the water on my body burned like chemicals."

"Did anyone ever counsel you during that time?" George asked.

"My family and neighbors talked to me about the problem. Even my fellow drinkers used to tell me, 'We all drink, but you have excelled on us.' They isolated me and made me sit on the ground. But with my stupidity and with Satan entering my brain, I didn't notice how bad things were.

"I wouldn't sleep until I had filled my bottle at the bar for the next morning. I would pay for it and put it on the table. By the time the Islamic call for prayer came at five in the morning, I was there knocking at the door. The bar owner would open the door, give me my bottle and three cigarettes, and go back to bed.

"Having sold off my bed and mattress, I was now just sleeping on old sacks. Eventually, my father locked the house because there wasn't anything left in it, and I was forced to sleep on a stack of bricks that I didn't have the firewood to burn. But truly, how could they let me sleep in the house? How could I fit in a family of the royal clan, me who looked like a mad person? My father refused to let me enter the house to eat, but even though my father refused, my mother would sneak food to me when she could."

"Now, I know you said that you don't have much time today. Let's talk about how you quit," George interjected, worried for Kajumba's beans and the fading sun.

"It was June 1999," Kajumba continued. "There was a crusade at the playing field and people singing a song in Swahili, 'Wa milele wa milele. Mungu wabaraka ni Yesu (Jesus is the eternal blessing).' As they sang, my heart started to pound in my chest.

"Two women from the church came over to me and said, 'Come to the gospel and Jesus will free you from alcohol.'

"I answered, 'Give me one week and I will get saved.'

"This wasn't the first time I had thought about this. My young brother was saved, and he was always telling me to get saved. And this was the time when my friends were seeing me as a nuisance and didn't want me near them. I didn't have any money left and had sold everything that I had. I had begun to realize that my drinking was a serious problem and had even told that young brother that I was going to jump in front of a car and kill myself. I had also started having strange dreams that left me weakened when I woke up.

"The next morning, I went to see the woman at the bar for my morning bottle, as I always did. That morning I drank and even brought some home, I don't remember what I had sold then to buy that bottle. I went to my stack of bricks, drank, and slept.

"When I drank on that particular day, I woke at around 3:45 p.m. and I saw the Lord. I can't say it was a dream, but I saw him. I woke abruptly, and I was sweating heavily. In the vision, the Lord was wearing clothes like a caterer."

"Like a chef?" George asked, thinking he had misheard.

"Exactly! He was up on wooden stairs, and I tried hard to reach him but couldn't. He said to me, 'Child, you have refused to leave alcohol, but I am here mending my shoes.' For sixteen years I have failed to interpret this vision. It could be that I didn't hear well, but that's what he told me.

"I woke up again a few minutes later, sweating heavily, and my heart was telling me, 'Go and get saved, otherwise you will die of alcohol.' I stood up. As I reached the water tank over there, my younger brother who had got saved before came. I told him, 'I am going to get saved. The Lord has asked me to get saved.' He doubted that I was serious, but he said, 'I will go with you.' He went and got his bicycle and drove me until we reached Christian Glory Center.

"At that time, the road to the church was still narrow and bushy, but Pastors Christopher, Charles, and Andrew were there. Pastor Christopher saw me from about thirty meters away and shouted to me 'You man, you really are blessed by God.'"

"Before he even knew you?" George asked.

Kajumba stopped talking and started to cry. George stopped talking too, and both men sat in the sitting room in silence for a few minutes as Kajumba's tears streamed down his face. After some time, Kajumba composed himself and continued.

"Pastor told me, 'You were about to die in just a matter of hours.' And it was the truth because I really was about to throw myself into the moving cars speeding down Entebbe Road. The pastor then asked, 'Why have you come here?' I said, 'Pastor, I have come to get saved.' He told Pastor Charles, 'Go and pray for that man.' Pastor Charles took me to the church, which was small at that time. Inside the church, we also found a niece of mine, another girl who was always asking me to get saved. When she saw me, her face lit up with joy and she said, 'Uncle has come to get saved!' Pastor Patrick began to pray for me and that is when I lost consciousness. When I woke up, my niece was still there, waiting for me.

"This was a Friday. Pastor Andrew was the first person who gave me clothes to put on the following Sunday. He also gave me a Bible. I, the person who never bathed, never shaved, realized at that time how filthy I was. Something big dispossessed me and then I realized how dirty I was. At home, I told my mother how I got saved. But she replied in a mocking voice, 'Got saved? Glory be to the Lord.' She thought it was a joke.

"[When I went to church on Sunday], the service bored me at first. [After the service], I went to Pastor Patrick, and he asked who I was. I told him, 'I am the man Kajumba who you prayed for.' He was amazed. He had thought I wouldn't stick to it, but indeed God had changed me instantly."

. . .

This story is a testimony. While Kajumba rarely shares it publicly, it is a narrative that is intended to convince us, and others who might be converted, that God can heal people and act in their lives. It is also intended to give praise, glory, and thanksgiving to a God to whom Kajumba himself remains deeply and sincerely devoted. As such, this story would find an easy place in one of the many slim glossy-covered devotional tracts published by both Ugandan and American pastors that one finds for sale on street corners and bookshops in Kampala. But what are we to do with such a story, here at the start of a book that is not a devotional text?

While Kajumba's story is indeed extraordinary, it is not at all unusual to hear such stories in Uganda. This is true both in the sense of the severity of the difficulties he faced because of his drinking and in the way he eventually escaped from those challenges. Problems that addiction researchers would term alcohol use disorders are common in Uganda. A recent study estimates that nearly 10 percent of adults in Uganda have an alcohol use disorder (Kabwama et al. 2016), and the per capita consumption rate among drinkers is among the highest in the world (World Health Organization 2014). However, as Kajumba's story reveals, biomedical models of these problems and of the pathways that might lead towards their resolution are not the only or even the dominant framework for understanding and addressing these issues.

As should already be clear, Kajumba's understanding of his transformation differs in significant ways from the prevailing biomedical model of addiction. Since the 1990s, clinicians, policymakers, and members of the public in many countries have increasingly been taught to think of addiction as a chronic relapsing brain disease (CRBD). Under the CRBD model, addiction is understood to be a problem of individual biology that results from the permanent effects of drugs and alcohol on a person's neural circuitry. This model both diverges from earlier stigmatizing models of addiction that centered on an individual's weakness of will (Valverde 1998) and replaces earlier clinical attempts to cure addiction through the use of various physical and chemical techniques (Campbell 2007). Importantly for the purposes of this book, the CRBD model also casts addiction as a problem that can be managed, but never cured. And so, while the idea that addiction is a disease rooted in biology might free a person from the stigma of earlier moralizing models focused on the will, the focus on chronicity certifies that one is consigned to a life of inescapable repetition, and this too may be a heavy burden to bear (Garcia 2010). In this book, we explore the affordances (Keane 2016) of ways of viewing and experiencing addiction and recovery that diverge from the CRBD model for Ugandans attempting to leave alcohol behind. While the idioms of deliverance, aversion, and possession that you will find in the chapters of this book are at times severe, we argue that they contain within them concepts and practices that point away from models of addiction as a chronic relapsing brain disease and towards the possibility of release.

Kajumba's story also presents an opportunity for anthropologists to broaden their understanding of processes of ethical transformation to better accommodate the effects of spiritual experiences and the diverse range of understandings of agency and ontology that underpin these experiences. In diverse contexts around the world, people's narratives of ethical transformation often involve the voices and actions of nonhuman others. God's voice is heard in prayer. Ancestral spirits enter the body and demand a response. Life-transforming guidance is received in dreams. Yet, with several key exceptions (Mittermaier 2012; Lambek 2010; Stonington 2020; Qu 2022), anthropologists working to understand processes of ethical transformation in anthropology have sidelined these aspects of people's stories. So, while some anthropologists have given careful thought to how cultural discourses and practices might produce spiritual experiences (Luhrmann 2012; Csordas 2002; Cassaniti and Luhrmann 2014), less is known about the effects of these experiences themselves. This book takes an agnostic approach to the actual sources of such experiences, seeking not to explore why such things happen, but rather what effects these experiences have in people's lives.

In so doing, we draw on four years of collaborative fieldwork with Ugandans working to reconstruct their lives after attempting to leave problematic forms of alcohol use behind. Given the relatively recent introduction of Western ideas of alcoholism and addiction, most of these people have used other therapeutic resources including herbal emetic therapies, engagements with spirit medium-ship, and forms of deliverance and spiritual warfare as they are practiced in Pentecostal churches. Each of these therapeutic forms is grounded on a different understanding of agency, the self, and the social, and these can have profound consequences for the forms of life and sociality that may follow an effort to stop drinking.

Practitioners of these various forms of healing not only hold radically different understandings of the causes of problem drinking, but these understandings are underpinned by different understandings of the nature of reality itself. A psychiatrist might look to the interactions between genetic and environmental factors and the long-term effects of substance use on the brain, while a Pentecostal pastor might see the same problem as resulting from the interference of a demon. These two not only disagree about the cause of the problem, but about the existence of demons and their effects in the world. That said, while a Pentecostal pastor and a spirit medium might both engage in a world where spirits and other intangible beings exist and can act as causal agents, they may fiercely disagree with one another about the nature of those beings and how one ought to relate to them. As you will see in the chapters that follow, while people sometimes engage in different medical and spiritual practices simultaneously or in sequence, they navigate this terrain with care and see their choices as having serious stakes for their spiritual and material safety.

In recent years, anthropologists have become increasingly interested in "taking seriously" the realities, the ontologies, of their interlocutors (Candea 2011; Holbraad and Pedersen 2017; Archambault 2016; De La Cadena 2010; Holbraad and Viveiros de Castro 2016). This book is in part an effort to explore what it might look like to do this with groups of people who radically disagree with one another on these most fundamental questions.

Finally, in attending to the fruits of these vernacular therapeutic forms, this book also argues for giving renewed attention to forms of indigenous medical and spiritual practice in the medical anthropology of Africa. While these therapeutic forms differ from one another in substantial ways, they all point towards possibilities for re-conceptualizing addiction, recovery, and ethics that may prove relevant well beyond Uganda.

DRINKING PROBLEMS

In 2007 and 2008, China and George were working together on her dissertation research on NGOs in the villages where George had grown up. Despite their varying areas of focus, most of the NGOs working in the subcounty claimed to be working with a "sustainable," "holistic" model that incorporated issues as disparate as small-scale enterprise, early childhood play, personal finance, sex education, malaria prevention, food storage, schooling, and nutrition into programs that could ideally be sustained without external funding through ongoing community volunteerism (Scherz 2014). Yet, despite this broad array of concerns, one topic that appeared again and again in the interviews and casual conversations China and George had with their neighbors was conspicuously absent. Alcohol use, abuse, production, and sale were central elements in the stories people told about why this or that child was in or out of school, why a particular old man had been abandoned by his children, or conversely why another family was prospering through the brewing of banana beer. Yet these situations did not find a ready slot on the holistic list of development interventions, a standard slate of "African problems." Food security, deforestation, corruption, education, AIDS, war, water, and malaria figured prominently on this list; alcohol abuse did not. When alcohol use was mentioned in conversations with NGO employees, it was framed as a reason not to engage with a particular person or family: "You can't give anything to that one, he'll just drink the money!" As you might imagine, this left many of the most vulnerable children in the community outside the purview of development interventions. At that time, the absence of interest in alcohol in development circles[2] was paralleled by relative silence in the medical community and in the Ugandan national media. Alcohol was not part of the way scholars, journalists, physicians, and development workers had learned to write and think about Africa (Wainaina 2005).

This is not because the high rates of alcohol consumption were unknown. As China grew increasingly interested in these forms of silence around drinking, she started searching for articles related to alcohol in Uganda during her occasional trips to Kampala's internet cafes. She quickly found several articles that cited a set of WHO statistics listing Uganda as having a per capita consumption rate of

19.47 L of pure alcohol per year, giving the country the highest per capita alcohol consumption rate in the world (World Health Organization 2004). The American magazine *Time* featured a story entitled "The Battle to Stop Drink from Destroying Uganda" (Gatsiounis 2010). *Vice* (2012) produced a documentary entitled "Uganda's Moonshine Epidemic." Yet neither these more spectacular forms of international media attention nor quotidian neighborhood conversations seemed to be filtering into government policy or NGO agenda-setting.

This lack of interest in alcohol was also surprising given the works of scholars including Justin Willis (2002), Simon Heap (1998), and Emmanuel Akyeampong (1997) who have written extensively on the role of alcohol in African political history. Reading their works, one finds alcohol use, production, and trade at the center of a wide range of colonial debates. In colonial Nigeria, customs duties from imported liquor made up more than half of state revenues in certain areas during the first half of the twentieth century and were at the center of fierce debates over the relative importance of temperance and treasury (Heap 1998; Olorunfemi 1984). In the colonies of Central, Southern, and Eastern Africa where the 1890 Brussels Act banned the importation of intoxicating liquors for African consumption, the regulation of domestic beer brewing, sale, and consumption were areas of intense contestation (Willis 2002; Crush and Ambler 1992). In South Africa, there were boycotts against the sterile methadone-clinic-like beer halls where beer was dispensed to Africans (La Hausse 1988). In Uganda, Kenya, Tanzania, and Ghana the consumption of unlicensed beer and gin figured as acts of both dissent and desperation (Willis 2002; Akyeampong 1997).

The first version of the project that became the book you are reading now was focused on trying to understand how it was that alcohol had fallen out of public debate and why it was that it had not returned. Yet, as China began to track this story at a distance by compiling a database of Ugandan newspaper stories related to alcohol with her undergraduates, something surprising started to happen. While it was not as though there was nothing about alcohol in the earlier papers, there was a marked shift in the number of articles referencing alcohol between 2007 and 2017. In 2007, the newspaper *The Monitor* featured 22 articles referencing alcohol; in 2017, there were 113. These articles covered a whole range of issues: traffic accidents, deaths from impurities in tiny plastic tot packs of waragi produced by unlicensed distillers, new packaging and promotions, the multinational drinks industry's growing interest in expanding its market share, and targeted attempts by the Ministry of Health and several emergent civil society organizations to generate media attention through the sponsoring of press conferences and workshops. Something was changing, if not in Ugandan society, at least in the Ugandan English-language print media.

There also seemed to be an increasing interest in substance abuse, mental health, and noncommunicable diseases among practitioners and scholars of global health (Beaglehole and Bonita 2009). A small but expanding number of studies were documenting linkages between high levels of alcohol consumption and morbidity and mortality from diseases like HIV (Bajunirwe, Bangsberg, and Sethi 2013; Wolff et al. 2006; Kagaayi et al. 2014; Karamagi et al. 2006; Kerridge et al. 2014; Kiwanuka et al. 2013; Ssekandi et al. 2012; Martinez et al. 2008; Mbulaiteye et al. 2000; Musinguzi et al. 2014), tuberculosis (Kirenga et al. 2015; Macintyre 2011), cancer (Cook 1971; Qian et al. 2014), and alcohol-related liver diseases (Schwartz et al. 2014). Researchers were also exploring links between excessive alcohol use and a variety of social problems including child maltreatment (Culbreth et al. 2021), intimate partner violence (Zablotska et al. 2009), and homelessness (Swahn et al. 2018).

Over time, we came to see these popular and scholarly articles as evidence of a larger process of problematization (Foucault 1997; Rabinow 2003), a process of defining and naming, of transforming unproblematized "difficulties" or "quasi-events" (Povinelli 2011) into problems that can be seen and addressed. The process of problematization takes the chronic, cruddy, cumulative, and corrosive aspects of life that "constitute "the 'slow rhythms' of lethal violence" (153) but which "never quite achieve the status of having occurred or taken place" (13). The process of problematization transforms these diffuse difficulties into a crisis that can be publicly addressed.

Statistics are often central to the process of transforming these quasi-events into more catastrophic ones that demand public attention (Povinelli 2011; Hacking 1990; Foucault 2009) and statistics certainly played such a role for researchers, health practitioners, and policymakers in Uganda as they attempted to draw attention to the severity of alcohol-related problems. Much of this process focused on the statistics on alcohol consumption in Uganda that the World Health Organization released as part of their 2004 Global Status Report on Alcohol, which China too had found back in that Kampala internet cafe. While this 2004 figure was likely based on a methodological error,[3] it was spectacular, and spectacles can take on a life of their own. When cited in local and international newspaper articles, documentaries, and television programs, this number had the capacity to transform the corrosive ordinariness of heavy drinking—the hangovers, the arguments, the emptied savings—into a per capita consumption rate that could be identified as an emergency capable of commanding national and international headlines. These statistics also laid the groundwork for the production of other more specific epidemiological data on the health effects of alcohol in Uganda, giving the researchers who contributed to the recent uptick of papers a powerful number to cite as they made their grant applications for these studies.

As you will see throughout this book, this process of problematization remains ongoing. In addition, the task of creating an audience eager to pursue the sorts of services provided in treatment centers and AA fellowships was, and remains, contingent on developing yet more specialized forms of awareness. Specifically, the survival of these programs is dependent on establishing "alcoholics," "addicts," and "people in recovery" as particular "kinds of people" (Hacking 1986), as people who can be classified as belonging to "definite classes with definite properties." This process also depends on convincing people of the benefits of engaging with the psy-professionals among the middle and upper classes (Vorhölter 2017).

As in other instances of "making up people," this process involves many players, not least of whom are practitioners of the human sciences such as medicine, psychology, and sociology. Through their efforts to count, correlate, and biologize, they engage in processes of discovery which not only describe but also radically transform the lives of those they seek to classify and understand. To be sure, much of the addiction research that is central to this process happened long ago, and far away from Uganda, in clinics, laboratories, prison farms, and communities in the United States (Campbell 2007). Indeed, little research on addiction treatment has been carried out in Uganda or anywhere in sub-Saharan Africa. Nevertheless, as we will discuss in greater depth in chapter 2, this way of "being a person" has been brought to Uganda by people living in Uganda, both Ugandans and expatriates, who were concerned about the problem drinking they saw around them and who had enough exposure to American models of addiction to think that they might be useful.

While tracking the emergence of this new field of practice is part of what concerns us in this book, as this project took shape another thing began to happen in our own thinking. As we lifted our gaze from what was, or was not, happening in the hospitals and NGOs, we soon realized that there was a great deal taking place around the problem of alcohol in other areas of Ugandan society. While drinking is certainly a socially acceptable practice in Uganda (Ssebunnya et al. 2020), distinctions between those who drink well and those who drink in ways considered to be problematic are also topics of whispered gossip and hot debate at places like the small roadside bars where we have been regular visitors since 2015. While there was indeed a growing level of public concern over alcohol use and addiction in Uganda, these conversations were happening without reference to these new terms and seemed to be anything but new.

In Luganda, the language most often spoken in the central region of Uganda and in the capital city Kampala, people whose drinking is seen as problematic may be referred to in these conversations as *omutamivu* (a drunkard), derided as *kanywa mugule* (a person who drinks while others buy for him), or gossiped about as *ekiwanga okusala leerwe* (a person whose head has crossed the railway tracks).[4] Most notably, given the importance of questions of self-control and agency in this book, men who drink in ways that are considered problematic may be derisively referred to and feminized by others with the saying *omwenge gwamuwasa* (alcohol has taken that man as his wife), implying that that person is now being controlled by alcohol in the way that a woman might be controlled by her husband. These categorizations imply an undesirable loss of self-control and self-rule (*okwefuga*), and are most often used when drinking leads to overspending on alcohol for oneself and others. Yet, despite the similarities between this purported loss of self-control and the metaphor of the hijacked brain common in American addiction discourse, these names point to something other than addiction and do not necessarily carry with them the idea of a chronic disease, rooted in biology, that is at once incurable and manageable.

THERAPEUTIC PATHWAYS

Even more important than our sense that alcohol-related problems were being spoken about in ways that exceeded the bounds of addiction discourse was our growing awareness that there were other ways of responding to these problems that were already operating in the "treatment gap" (Bartlett, Garriott, and Raikhel 2014). While a growing number of people seeking help for problems related to alcohol were enrolling in rehabilitation centers, others were seeking care outside of these institutions.[5] At its most basic level, this book is an attempt to explore the lived experience of people navigating a therapeutic ecology (Langwick 2008), which is both medically and religiously plural. Given the ways that life in Uganda is shaped by neoliberal ideas, we might do equally well to think of the relationships between these different therapeutic alternatives through the related metaphor of the marketplace.

In so doing, we describe the diverse explanatory models (Kleinman, Eisenberg, and Good 1978) through which different practitioners and patients come to understand and define situations in which alcohol has begun to create serious problems. While the specific treatments may differ, at a broad level these same four therapeutic pathways are often engaged as people work to resolve problems in their lives, including problems with other substances like tobacco, marijuana, and opioids and problems with addictive behaviors like gambling. People's engagements with these pathways also go well beyond substance use and may involve a wide array of medical, social, economic, and psychological issues.

Rehabilitation Centers

As we will discuss in chapter 2, several inpatient rehabilitation programs have emerged in Kampala over the past decade, but these programs still only reach a tiny fraction of the Ugandan population that has been estimated to be alcohol dependent. These centers include a government-funded thirty-day residential program offered to people with alcohol and drug addictions free of charge and a number of private clinics of varying levels of formality. These programs largely follow the Minnesota Model, applying principles drawn from Alcoholics Anonymous (AA) in an in-patient setting. Despite the low cost of the public center, most of the patients at inpatient rehabilitation centers in Kampala are male, speak English fluently, have attended university, and come from wage-earning families with relatively high incomes. Some former patients from these centers continue to see each other at Kampala's two AA meetings, and some have gone on to form an NGO dedicated to supporting Ugandans living in recovery. As is true in many contexts influenced by Euro-American models of addiction and recovery, individualistic models of the will, the self, and of personal responsibility are classic themes for staff members working at these sites. Patients are taught to take responsibility for their future actions, advised to cut ties with old friends, and encouraged to think about addiction as a genetically determined condition.

Herbal Medicine

In Uganda, almost every plant is used to treat at least one disease or ailment. In rural Central Uganda, most homes grow at least one plant for the medicinal properties of its leaves, bark, roots, flowers, or fruits. The most common ones treat fever, coughs, skin infections, and issues related to pregnancy and childbirth. Others might be used to treat fresh wounds, fractures, or sexual problems. Most commonly, green plants are squeezed to produce juice, and this juice is drunk or used for bathing to stop or prevent a disease.

In addressing alcohol-related problems, herbalists typically engage in a form of aversion therapy by providing patients with an emetic that can be added to either alcohol or water to induce an episode of violent and uncontrollable vomiting. Family members and friends sometimes administer this treatment without the patient's knowledge or consent. These emetics are produced from several different plant species, and the herbalists we have worked with each use slightly different formulations. In all cases, they have asked us not to name the specific plant species in our writings due to fears of exploitative bioprospecting (Hayden 2003; Osseo-Asare 2014). Respecting this request, we will not include the Kiganda or Latin names of specific plants in this work. The ingestion of this emetic is thought to induce a permanent aversion to alcohol by causing the patient to find its smell repulsive. Due to the scarcity of some of the plants used to produce this medicine, it is relatively expensive to purchase it; a single course of treatment might cost between 50,000–300,000 UGX or 15–60 USD. Even on the lower end, this amount might represent a significant portion of a month's income and would be considered a major purchase.[6]

Pentecostal Churches

Uganda is approximately 83 percent Christian (UBOS 2014), and religion features prominently in many aspects of everyday public and private life (Scherz 2014; Boyd 2015; Zoanni 2019; Eisenstein 2021). While Catholics and less-observant Anglicans drink openly, Pentecostals generally avoid alcohol, and the problems of excessive alcohol consumption are common topics in their church services and other prayer sessions. The approach to addiction found in these churches focuses on the theology and practice of spiritual warfare. Under the logic of spiritual warfare, all problems arise from the interference of Satan and other demons in people's lives. Helping people to overcome their problems requires that they learn how to uncover, release, and avoid "bondages" that allow Satan to bring problems such as alcoholism, poverty, and illness into their lives and the lives of members of their extended families. While scholars have often focused on the bounded individualism of Christianity, this understanding of spiritual warfare makes clear that this individualism can exist in tension with understandings of the self in which actions and character are deeply influenced by other people and spiritual beings (Daswani 2015; Bialecki and Daswani 2015; Coleman 2011). This way of thinking about addiction also differs substantially from the model put forward by Alcoholics Anonymous, and the disease model of addiction more generally, with regard to the question of permanence. In the disease model, addiction may be framed as something genetic, or something acquired, or some combination of the two, but whatever the cause it is seen as something permanent. By contrast, practitioners of spiritual warfare see addictions as potentially temporary.

Empewo

Most of the Pentecostals we have come to know through this study have complex, and often adversarial, relationships with practitioners of Uganda's traditions of indigenous healing—particularly when herbal medicines are combined with an engagement with what may be termed "powers" or *empewo* (literally, winds). In Buganda, specialists called *basamize* address a wide range of misfortunes.[7] Like the Pentecostals involved in the practice of spiritual warfare, they approach drinking problems through efforts to mediate the relations drinkers have with an array of beings that we might refer to as intangible persons (Thornton 2017), copresences (Beliso-De Jesus 2015), or special beings (Orsi 2018). Such spirits are thought to drink the alcohol owed to them through the bodies of those they possess. Yet where the Pentecostals seek to exorcise these spirits, the basamize seek to attend to these spiritual relations through ongoing and mutually beneficial forms of care.

. . .

As is the case for other maladies and misfortunes, people often sought out more than one of these methods, either simultaneously or in sequence. The paths that people trace between these various therapeutic alternatives are in part shaped by their religious commitments and their varied understandings of the compatibility between different medical and religious practices. While some of the Christians we met in the Pentecostal churches described the rituals of the basamize as spiritually dangerous acts that courted the demonic and sought to distance themselves from any association with these practices, some of the basamize whom we met in the shrines were also active members of their local churches. While our Muslim friend and driver, Noah, emphatically declined our invitations when we asked if he wanted to join us at the shrine, others centrally involved at the shrine also identified as practicing Muslims. When we noticed that they had not eaten the food served to them at the feast, it was not because they felt the food was spiritually dangerous, but because it was still light out and they were fasting for Ramadan. In seeking to understand how people navigate the diverse array of medical and religious practices in Kampala, perhaps the most important thing to remember is that there is no one way that people approach this question. One Catholic might feel relatively comfortable keeping a rosary next to a pipe created to send smoke up to the *balubaale*, while another Catholic might see such a pipe as a Satanic object that needs to be avoided at all costs. That said, what is perhaps common for many people across all of these stances is a sense that one needs to consider such questions with care, given the possible spiritual, physical, psychological, economic, and social consequences of error.

Further, as the people who shared their time with us navigated this vast and varied medical and religious terrain, they did not go alone, and their choices were shaped by those that walked with them. Their friends, family members, neighbors, and sometimes even the bar owners who sold to them helped to define their therapeutic trajectories. The efforts that family members and friends made to help those they were concerned about also exceeded these therapeutic spaces. Neighbors gave advice, counseled, and pleaded. Parents prayed, told their children to avoid particular groups of friends, and offered them opportunities to establish a more fruitful life by giving them land to work or a small business to run. That said, in the interest of highlighting the specific effects and affordances of each therapeutic pathway, we have pushed the long and winding quests through which people move between these spaces to the background. This process of sequential or simultaneous engagement with multiple therapeutic forms is something that has been thoughtfully engaged by numerous medical anthropologists (Whyte 1997; Janzen 1982; Langwick 2008), and further work in this area with regard to forms of addiction treatment discussed in this book or in other contexts would no doubt be welcome. Nevertheless, we have chosen to focus less on this process of movement than on the internal workings of each therapeutic model and the differences between them.

Finally, while we are sensitive to the problems of "fixing" a person in place in an ethnographic text (Garcia 2010) and quite compelled by writings which focus on doubt and uncertainty (Bubandt 2014; Meinert 2020), on the "moments when facts falter" (Stevenson 2014, 2), we are also aware of the certainty with which neuroscientific models of addiction operate. In the interest of mustering the degree of rhetorical force necessary to counter this, we have purposely chosen to foreground the certainty with which people engaged alternate treatment modalities. This choice also aligns with the sentiments of our interlocutors, most of whom felt quite certain about the truths at which they ultimately arrived—however much they might disagree with one another.

BEYOND THE CLINIC

Our attention to these varied therapeutic pathways takes us far outside of the hospitals and clinics that have become increasingly central in contemporary work on the medical anthropology of sub-Saharan Africa. As China has argued elsewhere (Scherz 2018b), much recent work in medical anthropology has focused on the anthropology of biomedicine, and this has been especially true of the anthropology of sub-Saharan Africa.[8]

Vernacular therapeutic practices were once a topic of great interest to anthropologists and historians[9] writing on medicine and healing in Africa. These works were central to important debates concerning questions of rationality (Evans-Pritchard 1937), foundational to the development of major schools of anthropological theory such as symbolic anthropology (Turner 1968), and crucial to anthropological understandings of how sociocultural orders are reproduced and transformed (Comaroff 1981). Into the 1990s, anthropologists were designing ethnographic studies that offered sophisticated analyses on the battles over truth and power that shape the ontological politics of healing in Africa (Langwick 2010). Yet, while many of the works researched in the 1990s were still making their way through the publication process well into the new millennium, research projects that were conceived and gestated after the turn of the millennium were far less likely to consider vernacular practices in ways and in spaces that are not already defined by the biomedical. With a few exceptions (Thornton 2017; Victor and Porter 2017; Igreja, Dias-Lambranca, and Richters 2008), many of which consider Christian rather than indigenous healing practices (Hannig 2017; Boyd 2015), we now rarely find non-biomedical practices described as part of lived therapeutic ecologies. While earlier works still have much to offer, one can neither assume that their descriptions are consistent with present practice, nor that present theoretical concerns would not cause an anthropologist to notice quite a different set of details.

The decreasing focus on vernacular healing in medical anthropology is by no means limited to sub-Saharan Africa. Much of the work done by medical anthropologists around the world is now focused on the lives of health workers, patients, and things in hospitals, clinics, and health-related NGOs (Lock and Nguyen 2010). This trend may be an unintended consequence of the otherwise laudable shift towards critical medical anthropology and its much-needed focus on the systems of power and structures of violence that operate both within and outside of medical systems to create health disparities (Das and Han 2015). It also reflects a growing division between medical anthropology and the anthropology of religion (Whitmarsh and Roberts 2016). Works such as those by Elizabeth Roberts (2012), Sherine Hamdy (2012), and Alice Street (2014) show us how non-biomedical ideas and practices shape the life of the clinic, but still, the clinic remains the site and limits the discussion of these elements to the ways that they appear in spaces already defined by biomedicine.

While biomedicine is clearly present and should not be ignored, attending to the ways that biomedicine articulates with vernacular healing practices has displaced other possible questions we might ask about those practices themselves. To be clear, we have no interest in questing after a pure or unadulterated version of "traditional" medicine, but there may be a great deal to be learned by exploring the more expansive sources of the fragments that appear in clinical spaces.

When anthropologists fail to do this, they leave open major gaps in our descriptions of the ways many contemporary Africans, both urban and rural, live in relation to the vernacular therapeutic offerings in their cities, towns, and villages. Anthropologists often tell our readers that the medical offerings are plural and that they are shifting, but in the most recent writings on medical care and healing in sub-Saharan Africa, the descriptions of biomedical and developmental spaces are typically far more detailed than the descriptions of more vernacular sites. We know from anthropologists of global health like Adia Benton (2015) that the coverage by biomedicine is radically uneven, focusing on some illnesses, while ignoring others. With that discrepancy in mind, we need scholarship that describes not only what happens to the few caught up in the biotechnical embrace (Good 2001), but also what happens to the people whose quests for therapy lie primarily outside of it. Given the contingency of global health funding in our current political climate, it may well be the case that the number of those who find themselves outside of the clinic is growing rather than shrinking.[10] Finally, if one of the key things we know about "traditional" healing practices in sub-Saharan Africa is that they are constantly changing (Obbo 1996), we cannot let older ethnographic and historical accounts serve as a substitute for contemporary ethnographic work when we refer to what may be happening outside of the clinic in the present.

Further, as Stacey Langwick has eloquently argued, questions concerning the status of traditional medicine are deeply political ones. They are questions related to a "highly politicized and intimate battle over who and what has the right to exist" (2010, 232). While medical anthropologists working in Africa have followed Langwick in noting the political stakes of colonial and postcolonial efforts to sever the phytopharmaceutical aspects of African medical systems from their more political and religious elements (Droney 2017; Adu-gyamfi and Anderson 2019), anthropologists have been markedly less careful about their own continued participation in the dividing practices (Latour 1991). Where medical anthropologists and medical historians were once concerned with a broad range of healing practices that blurred the lines between the physical, the spiritual, and the political, more recent works have tended to focus on various aspects of phytopharmaceutical research (Droney 2014; Osseo-Asare 2014). These works are important and may help us to better understand new realities on the ground, but they also leave out the vast majority of healers and patients who have no connection to such institutions. These healers' lives may also reflect new realities that merit our attention, but they are harder to see at a distance.

There are also other dividing practices at stake in contemporary ethnographic writing on hospitals and laboratories linked to questions of time, of tradition, and of modernity. Some of these works seem to say, "Look! Africans are modern too." These works, are, in this way, not so unlike the Manchester School ethnographies produced by the members of the Rhodes Livingston Institute in their celebrations of Africans embracing modern Western practices (Wilson 1942). In so doing, they assert, and helpfully and accurately so, the similarity, the coeval belonging (Fabian 1983), of certain sites in Africa and in the worlds of their readers, a group presumed to be students and faculty members at universities in the Global North. While there are certainly apartment complexes, shopping malls, NGO offices, and laboratories in Kampala that easily fit this pattern, there are also places like the shrines of the basamize you will meet in chapter 5. These shrines are not part of the past. They are also not only found in remote villages; the one that concerns us in this book is in the center of Kampala. We could tell you truthfully that many of those who spend their days there spend much of their time talking about their work as land brokers, pouring over sports betting sheets, and attempting to realize their aspirations for music video production contracts. We could tell you about one who proudly told us about his daughter's recent enrollment at Makerere University, where she was seeking her BA in chemistry. Yet, it is not these things that make these healers, and their patients, coeval members of your own time. They are part of your own time because they are presently living. That they also think deeply and live their lives in relation to spirits and rituals that medical anthropologists working in sub-Saharan Africa rarely write about anymore, does not make them less so, and their practices need not be *about* modernity to be *part of* modernity (Sanders 2003).

Part of the studied neglect of vernacular healing practices, such as those undertaken by the basamize, may be a fear of portraying Africans as essentially irrational or unmodern. But, like a second-wave feminism that asserted that women could, in fact, be just like men—thus implicitly elevating those characteristics that were associated with men—in our avoidance of this area of healing and harming, we also, subtly, and perhaps inadvertently, shore up the value and legitimacy of "modern" "Western" practices. Biomedicine certainly plays a role in contemporary African life, but if the next generation of medical anthropologists working in Africa becomes too firmly entrenched in the clinic, the discipline will miss out on the tremendous richness that African traditions, hybridity, and cosmopolitanism have historically provided for our thinking about the diversity of human practice and experience. Such work requires sustained engagement with local languages, with the history of anthropology, and with field sites that are less easily visible on maps or in the media. Overcoming these obstacles is not impossible, but doing so will require that anthropologists think carefully about which projects are worthwhile and why it is that they think so.

Finally, these erasures are problematic not only for the political and empirical reasons laid out above, but also for the pragmatic reasons long championed by anthropologists. Quite simply, vernacular healing practices in Africa may have much to teach us about how people anywhere might best respond to the illnesses that shape and cut short our lives. We must not only keep a critical eye on the social determinants of health, the inadequacies of biomedicine, and the global movements of pills and practitioners, we must also look to these vernacular systems as places to learn *from*—and this must be equally true of Africa as it is for Tibet, Nepal, China, or India. We often say that biomedicine discounts these practices, but in ceasing to devote our scholarly attentions to them, we implicitly do the same.

We have only begun to explore what these practices might have to teach us in terms of healing our bodies and minds. This may be especially important for those illnesses that biomedicine still is not particularly good at addressing, things like pain, addiction, and mental illness. While the global health apparatus is busy trying to export biomedical remedies for these conditions abroad (Watters 2010), even as the efficacy of these remedies has been questioned at home, medical anthropologists might be more involved in exploring how these conditions are approached in places where people have developed different ways of understanding and approaching them.[11] What, for example, might we learn from Duana Fullwiley's (2010) work on the management of pain in Senegal? What is it about the management of schizophrenia in Zanzibar (McGruder 2004) that leads to increased wellbeing among sufferers and their families? How might practices related to the care of plants and people create new spaces of habitability in an increasingly toxic world (Langwick 2018)? As these citations indicate, there is already some work that hints at these potentials, but there is room for so much more.

Likewise, while a few works in the anthropology of addiction have looked at alternate ways of conceptualizing and addressing substance use disorders, the general decline in the scholarly energy dedicated to non-biomedical healing traditions in medical anthropology has also shaped much of the anthropological work in this field. In the earliest phase of work on substance use in anthropology, anthropologists were so focused on describing situations in which drinking was not constituted as a problem (Douglas 1987; M. Marshall 1979) and on the surprisingly wide range of ways that drinking shaped behavior (MacAndrew and Edgerton 1969; Heath 1995), that some worried that the field was ignoring what might, in fact, be serious alcohol-related problems in the communities under study (Room 1984). Since that time, anthropologists studying addiction have shifted their approach to focus on the limits of the universalizing medicalized vision of addiction as an individualized pathology. Most have done this by following Merrill Singer (1986; see also Singer et al. 1992) in analyzing the social determinants of substance abuse.[12] Other anthropologists and historians have focused on tracing the genealogy of contemporary biomedical addiction discourses (Valverde 1998; Campbell 2007; Netherland and Hansen 2016a, 2016b; Raikhel and Garriott 2013) and exploring how this discourse is altered as it moves across cultural contexts (Raikhel and Garriott 2013; Borovoy 2005; Brandes 2002; Prussing 2011; Harris 2016). In writing this book, we join a small but growing number of scholars who have sought to explore what lies in the "treatment gap" (Bartlett, Garriott, and Raikhel 2014). These scholars have drawn attention to the contingency of medicalized approaches to addiction by exploring other ways of conceptualizing and responding to problems related to substance use (Gamburd 2008; Spicer 2001; Raikhel 2016; Garcia 2010; Hansen 2018; O'Neill 2019; Bartlett 2020). In focusing our efforts on understanding other ways of living life after alcohol, we want to think about the ways that these alternatives might offer generative visions for an otherwise view (Zigon 2018; Povinelli 2011; Robbins 2013) to the dominant chronic relapsing brain disease model.

ETHICS, AGENCY, ONTOLOGY, AND EXPERIENCE

Beyond these concerns related to medical anthropology and the anthropology of addiction, this is also a book that aims at intervening in conversations about the anthropology of ethics, agency, ontology, and experience. Like so many of the stories we heard over the course of our time talking with people about their efforts to leave drinking behind, Kajumba's story hinges on a dream, a vision. His vivid half-waking encounter with God—dressed as a caterer and mending his shoes, calling him to get saved—crystalized a series of happenings that came before and pushed him towards the series of social and supernatural interventions that followed. Before the vision, there was Kajumba's father throwing him out of the house, his near-suicidal despair over the condition of his life, his brother asking him to get saved, his heart beating while hearing the song at the crusade, and his promise to the two women who approached him. These were all key elements in his transformation. After the vision, there was the pastor who recognized him as he approached the church, his brother's willingness to drive him on his bicycle, the appearance of his niece, Pastor Patrick's prayer of deliverance, his loss of consciousness, and Pastor Andrew's gift of the shirt. While the more social elements of the before and the after are fairly comfortable ground for social scientific analysis, the more miraculous elements, such as the vision itself, are things we are less likely to encounter in writings on ethico-moral transformations.

Had Kajumba focused his story on a series of daily practices through which he worked to transform himself into a new kind of person, we would have a clear sense of where to look in the anthropological literature for analytical tools. Over the past fifteen years, anthropologists studying processes of ethical transformation have focused on moments of evaluative reflection and intentional projects of self-cultivation. These scholars have all used Michel Foucault's later works (Foucault 1990; 2005) as a model for illuminating the ways that people take up particular exercises of self-cultivation in an effort to align their desires, habits, and actions with various moralities and understandings of the good (Mahmood 2004; Faubion 2011; Robbins 2004; Rabinow 2003; Zigon 2011; Scherz 2013). Yet, while the focus on intentional action and reflexive thought that characterizes this approach has provided a helpful corrective to overly determinist frameworks for the study of morality and social life more generally (Laidlaw 2013), it also comes with certain limitations. Specifically, in this effort to better incorporate freedom, deliberation, and projects of intentional self-making, scholars have tended to background other aspects of ethical life and personhood that are less easily controlled (Scherz 2018a).

Among these less controllable aspects are various forms of spiritual experience and the divinities or other spiritual beings who often appear as agents in people's narratives of ethical transformation. The possibility that such beings are involved in collectivities capable of shaping the self has received only occasional attention (Mittermaier 2012; Lambek 2010; Stonington 2020; Laidlaw 2013; Scherz and Mpanga 2019; Scherz 2018a; Qu 2022). This lack of focus is surprising given both people's explicit articulations of divine action as an explanation for personal moral transformations (Daswani 2015) as well as the current disciplinary interest in questions of ontology and phenomenology.

Attending to accounts of the role of spiritual experience in processes of ethical transformation, such as Kajumba's, is a difficult task for several reasons. As noted earlier, there are problems presented by anthropologists' use of the anthropology of ethics to highlight the character and place of freedom in settings poorly served by models that privilege either slavish obedience to culture or unmediated acts of resistance (Laidlaw 2002; Mahmood 2004). Despite other points of divergence among scholars working in this area, there is a sense of agreement that to study ethics is to study the intentional, the conscious, and the reflective. Scholars working on the anthropology of ethics have often focused on the importance of the process of both conscious reflection and intentional action, whether considering moments of moral breakdown among former heroin users in post-Soviet Russia (Zigon 2007, 2008, 2011), the moral experiments of African American parents of children with serious medical problems in Los Angeles (Mattingly 2014), Cairene women participating in Islamic piety movements (Mahmood 2004), the sudden moments of self-awareness and critique that punctuate the lives of frontline community psychiatry workers (Brodwin 2013), or the moral torment of Christians in Papua New Guinea (Robbins 2004). This scholarly work has no doubt provided a helpful corrective to overly determinist frameworks. Yet in this otherwise laudable focus on freedom, we might be drawn dangerously close to a view of the subject as a self-determined individual who experiences, perceives, and lives in relation to a world of others without being directly entered or affected by them.

Attending to accounts in which God, balubaale, or other spiritual beings play significant roles in the constitution of ethical subjects also raises a series of difficult questions about agency and ontology. In short, we have had to decide whether to write of those beings as agents capable of influencing the world directly, or whether we will write only about the effects of the beliefs and practices that people have constructed in relation to them. While many of our interlocutors were deeply committed to explanations that saw spiritual beings as responsible for a given person's struggle with alcohol, as scholars we are still left to decide whether we will write about the effects of the way that that circle of responsibility is drawn (Laidlaw 2013) or about the effects of those beings themselves.

Over the course of the past seven years of research and writing (Scherz 2017, Scherz and Mpanga 2017, Scherz, Mpanga, and Namirembe 2022), we have found ourselves pulled between these two modes of engagement. On the one hand we felt drawn to consider perspectives that would allow us to move beyond an understanding of spiritual experience focused on the rhetorical influence of ritual speech (Csordas 1997) and the human practices that kindle such experiences into existence (Cassaniti and Luhrmann 2014; Luhrmann 2012). We took to heart Dipesh Chakrabarty's (1997) critiques of the disenchanted world of the social sciences and hoped that writings of those identified with the ontological turn (Candea 2011; Holbraad and Pedersen 2017; Archambault 2016; De La Cadena 2010; Holbraad and Viveriros de Castro 2016; Kohn 2015) or indigenous anthropology (Watts 2013; Todd 2016; Bawaka Country et al. 2016; Tallbear 2017) might provide us with a path that would allow us to more fully consider the world as our interlocutors did. Yet, as we will discuss in the conclusion, it may not only be disenchanted social scientists (Chakrabarty 1997) who would be nervous about a book that contained assertions about the agency of spiritual beings. We will return to this question throughout the coming chapters in various ways, but for now, we simply invite you to see what becomes possible and impossible, visible, and invisible, as you shift between thinking about the effects of belief, ritual, and human sociality and the effects of spiritual beings themselves.

HOW WE WROTE THIS BOOK

Life in Uganda has inclined all three of us to convert material wealth into carefully composed networks of relationships whenever we can. As we will discuss in greater depth in the chapters that follow, it is next to impossible to do anything in Uganda without relying on a dense network of relational ties. While the role of relationships in addiction recovery is central to the content of this book, at a more methodological level this book is also an outcome of such a materially mediated relational composition. In taking this approach, we are bringing insights drawn from Uganda and elsewhere in Africa about the ethics of interdependence (Kopytoff and Miers 1977; Guyer 1995; Scherz 2014; Hanson 2003; Comaroff and Comaroff 2001; Ferguson 2013; Cole and Thomas 2009; Zoanni 2018) into the rapidly expanding conversation in the need for more collaborative forms of anthropological practice (Deger 2006; Bejarano et al. 2019; Lassiter 2005), and, in the process, helping to transform a long history of important, but largely invisible, contributions made by assistants and translators in Africanist anthropology (Schumaker 2001).

As mentioned above, George and China's collaboration began in 2007, when China was just starting her dissertation research on orphan support programs in Uganda. At that time, she hired George to work for her as a translator and research assistant, and together they explored the workings of an orphan support program operating in his home village. Through that project, they developed a collaborative relationship that became the basis for this book. By the time they started working together again on this project in 2015, George had completed his BA at Kampala International University and had also worked as an assistant for several other historians and anthropologists including Jon Earle, Emma Wildwood, Erin Moore, Edgar Taylor, Jacob Dougherty, and Tyler Zoanni. When China asked George to join her in working on this new project about alcohol, she suggested that instead of working as an assistant on the project, he might work as a full collaborator and that they would try to coauthor most of the writings that came out of the project—including the book you are reading.

An initial startup grant from the University of Virginia allowed China to hire George to work on the project on a full-time basis. At the outset, George and China worked alongside one another, both taking notes on the same events and then comparing them afterwards. After the first nine weeks of working in this way, China returned to the United States, and George carried on with the fieldwork in between China's visits to Uganda. During these periods apart, China reviewed and coded transcripts using the web-based mixed methods software Dedoose. The two then met over Skype for two to four hours a week to discuss the notes, transcripts, and their plans, progress, and emerging ideas about the shape of the project.

In February 2018, China received a grant from the National Science Foundation (Award #1758472). This grant not only allowed George and China to continue their work, but also allowed them to hire and train an additional collaborator, Sarah Namirembe. Sarah and George grew up in the same village and had known one another since Sarah was a young girl. George was a friend of Sarah's family and often visited her when she was away at school. It was thus to their mutual delight when we ran into her by chance when she was serving as a volunteer educator in the Alcohol and Drug Unit at the National Psychiatric Hospital. Once she joined the project, Sarah went through a similar training process both with China and with George, learning how to take field notes and conduct interviews. George (July 2015–July 2019) and Sarah (January 2018–July 2019) conducted fieldwork on a full-time basis. China joined the team in Uganda for a total of twenty-four weeks spread over the course of the four years.

Our team has also included our friend Noah Wabwiire, who worked as our driver, our tech support specialist, and later our transcriptionist. We also worked with a number of University of Virginia and Reed College undergraduates including Aubrey Bauer, Emily Weisenberger, Claire Mooney, Likita Griffith, Priscilla Opoku-Yeboa, and Beza Bogale. Most of these students worked with China to build and maintain a coded database of more than eight hundred news articles discussing alcohol drawn from the Ugandan English language print media. Our team in Uganda was also joined by two additional undergraduates, Anne Nelson Stoner and Amber Colby. China and George supervised these students as they conducted six weeks of fieldwork at a Pentecostal church and an inpatient rehabilitation center during the summer of 2017. Anne Nelson also returned for an additional nine weeks of followup fieldwork in 2018.

During the four years of our fieldwork we spent time and spoke with nearly three hundred people in bars, rehabilitation centers, Alcoholics Anonymous fellowships, churches, herbalist clinics, and shrines. The vast majority of this work took place in Uganda's capital city, Kampala. Kampala has a population of approximately 1.5 million people, with an additional one million commuting into the city for work each day. Given the number and variety of available options, including the country's two major inpatient rehabilitation programs, it provided us with an excellent location for exploring the range of treatment modalities currently available in Uganda.

Given our interest in the ways that processes of personal transformation play out over time, most of our efforts were focused on following twenty-one people who had or were trying to stop drinking. While many of these people had had experience with multiple treatment pathways, they were each primarily involved in one form of treatment at the time of the study. In following this cohort we drew on observations, semi-structured interviews, and the coconstruction of illness narratives. Most importantly, we simply spent time with them, finding them at home, at work, and out with their friends. We were also frequent participants in addiction awareness and fundraising events, church services, educational sessions in rehabilitation centers, rituals held by basamize, and trips to gather herbal medicines in markets and forests.

Our methods, built as they were around following people home as opposed to interacting with people only as they were passing through therapeutic sites for treatment, were explicitly designed to move away from thinking about medical anthropological field sites as defined by institutions. While having a regular "place to go" provides an expedient boundary—something that may be especially welcome in the context of urban fieldwork—we used institutions as starting places but primarily sought to explore the lives of people as they moved beyond the moment of therapeutic encounter. We did this by letting people, rather than sites, define the boundaries of the study.

This process of working together across a wide range of sites has transformed the project into something that none of us could have created independently of the others. At a very basic level, the collaborative nature of the project has allowed us to collect data at a much wider range of sites and over a much longer and more uninterrupted period of time than would have otherwise been possible. At a deeper level, and perhaps more importantly, working collaboratively has allowed us to think about the things we have learned during our fieldwork from different perspectives. Our positions, and our bodies, are read differently by those involved in our research, and this changes what people tell us and how we think about it. When we exchange field notes written about the observations we have made while standing side by side, we often find that we have noticed different things and come to different conclusions about them. China is a white, female academic from the United States. George is a man from Uganda. The fact that he is a father of twins with involvements in Buganda government affairs, clan leadership, and opposition party politics also changes things for certain people. Sarah is a young Ugandan woman with a BA in community psychology. She is also much more of an insider than either George or China in both the rehabilitation centers discussed in chapter 2 and the churches discussed in chapter 4. All of this changes how she relates to people in these spaces, and in others as well. Because of the racial hierarchies that continue to structure life in the postcolonial nations of Africa (Pierre 2012), China's position as a white academic meant that we were regularly granted meetings with senior hospital administrators, researchers, and Ministry of Health officials (see Covington-Ward 2016; Nannyonga-Tamusuza 2005). But the people involved in the study told George and Sarah things about their lives that they might well have hesitated to share with China. China's knowledge of anthropological theory led her to ask questions that will have relevance to current academic debates, but it was George and Sarah's depth of lived cultural, linguistic, and historical knowledge that often helped us to make sense of the answers.

This method also allowed us to have a series of conversations about how we wanted to write about the things we have learned. As we will address in greater depth in the conclusion, we have, for example, had many long discussions about how to engage with the claims made by healers and pastors concerning the nature and reality of the spirits who enter the bodies of those who frequent shrines. This question inflected our conversations about what implicit and explicit theoretical positions we wanted to take in our writing, and it also inflected our conversations about how to act within spaces like churches and shrines. Talking honestly about our interpretations of the different things we have seen and experienced helped us to better understand the array of approaches people might take to engaging with spirits– and also to better understand the stakes of different kinds of claims concerning the reality of spirits for differently situated people.

This process of cowriting has also afforded us an opportunity to foreground Ugandan perspectives. While there is no one "Ugandan" way of thinking, we have made it part of our collaborative practice to foreground our research participants' own frames of analysis as often as possible. This has involved taking the relevant sections of this book back to the people about whom we have written. Reading the sections aloud, often in Luganda translation, and seeking their feedback has been an invaluable process. In this review process, the people who you will read about in the chapters that follow have added crucial details to their stories that they had left out in earlier versions. They corrected our interpretations and challenged us to write with words and intention that correspond to their own understandings of the world. Working together as a team has made it easier for us to grasp these multiple Ugandan ways of seeing the world. It has also kept us accountable to this goal, if only by making us aware of moments when we chose to do something else.

Writing together also changed how we write in other ways. By coproducing texts from the first writing of field notes to the final draft of this book, writing together allowed us to consider and address questions of accessibility and voice that will ultimately change our readership. Writing together put questions about who and what anthropological writing is for at the center of our work. These questions led us to produce a broader range of writings and other research products. One of these, a twelve-part radio series coproduced in Luganda with CBS-FM Radio Buganda, has been primarily oriented to Ugandans who have not had the opportunity to attend university. We also hope that this book will be relevant to readers both inside and outside of Uganda and that our collaborative writing process has made us mutually accountable to this goal and given us a stronger sense of what might be relevant to these different audiences.

WHAT LIES AHEAD

The heart of this book is comprised of four ethnographic chapters that explore the four types of therapeutic sites in turn. In each of these chapters, the narratives of the people we have worked with are central and offer an opportunity to see how these different modes of conceptualizing and experiencing the self, and their relationships with an array of human and nonhuman others, have shaped their efforts to move towards a life after alcohol.

Before reaching those chapters, chapter 1, "*Batuzaala mu Baara*," discusses the history and social life of alcohol in Uganda. In it we explore the history of alcohol use and regulation in Uganda and the forms of social life that bars make possible.

Chapter 2, "Once an Addict . . . ," takes us into two of Uganda's formal inpatient rehabilitation centers–one public and one private. Within these spaces a new set of identities and ways of being in the world are taking shape. Through daily routines, private counseling sessions, and didactic trainings, some of which were led by Sarah herself before she joined our research team, the clients of these centers are being taught to understand themselves and those around them in radically new ways. Through the story of a young man named Maurice, we explore how trust, class, and new forms of biosocial belonging and isolation intersect with the disease model of addiction as it has been introduced to Uganda.

Chapter 3, "Put Something in His Drink," begins to move us beyond the clinic to the shop of an urban herbalist who treats alcohol-related problems with a form of emetic aversion therapy. Through an analysis of the life history of one of her clients, Mayanja, we explore the affordances of a form of treatment which transforms a person's embodied perception of the world, but which does not prescribe a transformation of one's social ties. Given this, people like Mayanja who stopped drinking through herbal medicine found it relatively easy to maintain their social ties with former drinking companions and generally continued to go to bars to socialize and drink highly caffeinated nonalcoholic beverages like Mountain

Dew and Rock Boom. We explore the effects of their relatively uninterrupted identities and networks of social support in and contrast it with the "total break" prescribed by Pentecostals and addiction counselors alike.

In chapter 4, "Not You," we turn to consider models of spiritual warfare and deliverance as they orient understandings of addiction in a Pentecostal fellowship in Kampala. Within these churches, people are taught to understand addictions as the result of the actions of demonic spiritual forces in their lives. As is also true of the practitioners of *kusamira* you will meet in chapter 5, members of these churches see some cases of problem drinking as caused by spiritual forces. For these Christians, moving beyond problems with alcohol requires them to exorcise the spirit which is causing the problem through deliverance. We argue that despite the apparent severity of the spiritual warfare discourse, this way of understanding addiction leads the members of these churches to see people as fundamentally separable from the spirits that might cause them to drink, and that this understanding creates important opportunities for people to begin again.

In chapter 5, "Call and Response," we focus on a community of basamize who participate in the form of mediumship and worship known as kusamira. While they also see some drinking problems as resulting from the influences of spiritual forces, for them the task is not deliverance, but rather finding ways to better accommodate the spirits by recognizing them and moving into a more productive relationship of reciprocity and mutual care. At both church and shrine, alcohol-related problems can be explained as resulting from the actions of an external force. Where they differ, and here they differ strongly, is about the moral valence of these external spirits and what ought to be done about them.

In the conclusion, finally, we attend to the theoretical challenges and insights that arose in this attempt to explore multiple sites where people have conflicting claims about therapeutic efficacy and about the things, beings, and substances that exist in the world: their natures, their effects, and the relationships between them. We explore how people navigate an array of competing and often conflicting claims to efficacy and how anthropologists might consider the possibilities and limits of the discipline with regard to these questions.

Throughout, our explorations of these varied therapeutic pathways speak to the importance of returning engagements with vernacular therapeutic forms to the center of medical anthropology and to carefully considering the role that spiritual experiences play in processes of ethical transformation. With regard to the latter point, this book considers how the transformative potential of spiritual experiences is shaped by a community's belief in the possibility of transformation, by its willingness to accept that things truly could be different. The collective faith that someone might truly be transformed opens up radically new possibilities for the incorporation of people into new communities of care and relationship. These new relationships are imperative given the importance of relationships in Uganda and the central role that bars play in their constitution and maintenance. Before moving forward with our discussion of how these different conceptualizations of the self and the social shape the various pathways out of problem drinking, we first turn to consider the forms of sociality that take shape around bottles of beer, jerry cans of *umkomboti*, plastic tot packs of waragi, and pots of *malwa* in the small bars lining so many of Kampala's roads.

1

Batuzaala mu Baala

Seeking Connection and Flow in Kampala's Bars

BATUZAALA MU BAALA

In the days surrounding Uganda's 2016 presidential election, the Ugandan musician Daxx Kartel's newly released song "*Baatuzaala mu Baala*" (We were born in bars) was enjoying widespread popularity.[1] Its danceable rhythm was used to call potential supporters to campaign rallies of all political parties, and it served as an apolitical compromise song that could be played in bars otherwise divided by patrons paying to play President Museveni's "*Tubonga Naawe*" (We stand with you) or, alternately, Besigye's opposition song "*Toka kwa Barabara*" (Clear the way). During these tense days of conflict and anticipation, "We Were Born in Bars" afforded temporary opportunities for release and served to create patches of common ground.

In this chapter, we use this song and the role it played in the 2016 election as a starting point for thinking about the historical, social, and experiential aspects of drinking in Uganda. While we would not want to take a functionalist stance, understanding the role that alcohol plays in daily life allows us to better comprehend the stakes of certain forms of sobriety in Uganda. To appreciate what it might mean to try to stop drinking, we have to first come to terms with what, beyond the alcohol, is at stake in movements toward sobriety. With this in mind, in this chapter we put recovery to the side, and focus on the bars themselves and the opportunities they provide for friendship, connection, and movement.

In contemporary Kampala, bars serve as the primary public site for social connection, and this is especially true for men. Bars are spaces of pleasure, friendship, and possibility. They are places for mobilizing social projects and talking politics. They are also crucial sites for connecting to job opportunities—a point that we've found to be equally important to brick makers and business lawyers. It would be easy to see a group of men seated at a roadside bar as embodying stasis and subject them to the same forms of judgment that afflict the youth who sit in the tea *fadas* of Niger. There, elders describe the lives of youth who sit and drink tea together with the evocative phrase *"kaman kasha wando,"* "the sitting that kills the trousers" (Masquelier 2019, 1). In this chapter, we follow Adeline Masquelier in showing how spaces that seem to be shaped by forms of endless waiting, immobility, and powerlessness can figure as important spaces of belonging and experimentation which enable people "to carve provisional spaces of existential possibility in the face of severely narrowed futures" (4). We show that the bar is experientially and pragmatically seen by these drinkers as a place of movement and flow. It is not only the pleasure that follows as beer and *waragi* flow from bottle to glass to body, but also the pleasure of the flow of money itself in a world where a strict logic of economizing dominates most other spheres of life. There is also the flow of people, friends and strangers alike, who have found themselves there at the bar, looking to get out of the house, to breathe some different air for a while. Between these people, words, ideas, and opportunities flow and people are released—if only for a few hours—from the pressures and tensions of everyday life.

DRINKING HISTORIES

Before moving on to discuss the contemporary place of alcohol in Ugandan society, it is worth pausing for a moment to see how the political, economic, and social history of Uganda shaped patterns of production, sale, and consumption over time. Historians and anthropologists writing on the place of alcohol in precolonial Africa have often described systems that largely restricted access to a limited supply of alcohol to a group of male elders and ancestors who were in turn responsible for ensuring well-being (Willis 2002; Colson and Scudder 1988; Akyeampong 1997). Across much of East Africa, male elders drank in age-restricted groups. Women and youth were only permitted to drink with their permission, and in some cases literally through their straws (Willis 2002, 71).

While beer was still tightly linked to power, the situation differed in the kingdoms of Buganda, Bunyoro, Toro, and Nkore, where multiple forms of power and methods for ensuring well-being were in simultaneous operation (Hanson 2009). Here, beer made by men from fermented banana juice called *tonto* was not limited to groups of elderly agemates. Instead, young kings (*bakabaka*) and other leaders (*batongole*) used beer to recruit and maintain armies of young men, allowing them to use coercive force to expand their kingdoms (Willis 2002, 80–86). The emergence of caravan routes in the nineteenth century provided opportunities for multiple forms of trade and ran alongside the trade in slaves and ivory; it similarly created new possibilities for power and for the sale and distribution of beer. *Tonto* was available as barter for cloth by 1891 and available for cash purchase as early as 1906 (Willis 2002, 91–94). As new sources of power and drink emerged over the decades that followed, questions concerning who would be allowed to drink became even more acute.

Understanding the dynamics of alcohol production, consumption, and sale in the first half of the twentieth century in East Africa also requires that we understand that East Africa lay in a region delineated as an "uncontaminated zone" in the 1890 Brussels Act. This situation can be contrasted with the situation in much of West Africa where European liquors known as "trade spirits" had been introduced as a form of currency during the slave trade and where the colonial state depended heavily on revenues generated through import taxes on spirits produced in Europe and North America (Akyeampong 1997). While the introduction of imported trade spirits was prohibited in Uganda, colonialism brought with it a host of changes to the material culture and legal system; this had unintended consequences for local practices related to the production, consumption, and sale of alcohol.[2]

Over the course of the first decades of the twentieth century, brewing for sale became an increasingly popular strategy for people who had to meet colonially imposed cash expenses like taxes and school fees. While tonto produced and sold by men would remain the most popular form of alcohol for some time to come, the distilled spirits known as waragi and *enguli* would eventually come to take its place among both male and female sellers. Distilled alcohol was unknown in Uganda before the mid-nineteenth century. In the early twentieth century, small scale production and distribution among soldiers was tolerated, but after the British accession to the Treaty of St.-Germain in 1919, the protectorate government passed new laws that aimed at not only more tightly regulating the production and sale of *tonto* but also at prohibiting Africans from consuming any spirits (Willis 2002). This law had unintended effects on the market in waragi. As the colonial government increased its ability to enforce the regulations and licensing fees they had put into place to control the production and sale of tonto, tonto production gradually became a less profitable enterprise. People began to look for a better option, and many, especially women, found an answer in waragi. As opposed to tonto, which spoils after a few days, making it unsuitable for storage and long-distance transport, waragi is highly concentrated and can be moved easily over long distances. These same qualities also mean that it can easily be hidden and smuggled, making its illegality less of an issue. Finally, since women could not legally produce and sell tonto, they largely left the tonto market to men and instead chose to take up the illegal production and sale of waragi. During this period, distilled spirits, including the waragi that these women were making and selling, were also becoming an increasingly important symbol of power, status, and modernity among local political and economic elites. Their consumption of imported and locally distilled spirits also became an issue of increasing concern to the colonial government,

leading to new ordinances, higher fines, longer prison sentences, and more frequent raids, but these initiatives had little effect, and the market for informally
distilled waragi continued to expand (Willis 2007).

After the Second World War, colonial governments in East Africa began to
shift tactics with regard to alcohol. In 1947, the government of Uganda granted
Africans the right to buy bottled beer in an effort to create a stable black elite that
would simultaneously replace Europeans as the consumer base for commercially
produced beer in the colonies and, more importantly, steady British control in
East Africa. In the following years, colonial rhetoric increasingly cast bottled beer
consumption as an important sign of modernity, relegating traditional fermented
drinks like tonto to an unhygienic backward past. Through their consumption
of European style bottled beer, a small Ugandan elite was being courted by the
British and being encouraged to further distinguish themselves from other Ugandans through these new drinking practices. While bottled beers were generally
sharply distinguished from spirits, imported spirits also came to play a similar
role in lubricating carefully orchestrated rituals of racial mixing among European
and African civil servants in the 1940s. In these spaces of privileged consumption,
Europeans sought to create narrow openings through which a small number of
Africans could use their enactment of European definitions of cultural refinement
to access a certain form of modernity and power.

Yet, the new laws around bottled beer and the meticulous staging of multiracial
sundowners did little to address the ever-growing colonial concerns over informally produced waragi, which offered access to "a kind of modernity not mediated
by Europeans" (Willis 2002, 226). In 1949, the government of Uganda charged a
committee with the task of investigating the waragi trade. Their report, produced
in 1951, fundamentally redefined the nature of the problem by narrowing the focus
on the toxins and fluctuating potency of illicit distillates and by carving out a new
possibility for modern formally-produced distilled spirits that went far beyond
the gradualism of earlier regulatory attempts. In this way, Justin Willis writes, the
"report was firmly located in a new debate about how the developmentalist postwar state should manage African contact with modernity, in which alcohol played
an important part" (2007, 82).

The recommendations of the report were carried forward by Andrew Cohen,
who became governor of Uganda in 1952. In 1955, and in violation of both the
Brussels Act and the Treaty of St.-Germain, Cohen succeeded in his attempts to
change the law prohibiting Africans from buying spirits in Uganda. Yet, given the
price of European spirits, this change in the law did little to change illicit distillation practices or drinking patterns. Given the limited impact of this legal solution, Cohen went on to propose a local distillery capable of producing "a clean
spirit at a competitive price" (Willis 2007, 83). Cohen also thought that commercial
alcohol production could boost the sugarcane industry. The government in Kenya,

however, feared that domestically manufactured spirits would threaten the colonial economy due to the loss of import duties. This opposition made it impossible for Uganda to move forward with its plan.

Following independence in 1962, Uganda was free to put these disagreements with Kenya aside and established a new committee of inquiry under the leadership of Eriya Babumba. In an effort to balance his desire to provide people with a safe alternative to informally distilled waragi with the need to avoid alienating the vast network of Ugandans involved in the waragi economy, Babumba, inspired by models in Ghana and Sierra Leone, devised a system whereby informal enguli producers would be able to sell their product to a central distillery for redistillation and bottling. This system was codified in the 1965 Enguli Act, a document that redefined Waragi, capital W, as a commercially distilled spirit that was fundamentally different from the informally produced distillate enguli.

While the first bottles of Uganda Waragi were shipped out for sale in May 1965, the system ultimately did little to quell the informal trade in enguli. There were few licenses available, and the amount the distillery could purchase was very limited. Further, producers found they could charge local consumers less than half of what they would be charged for a bottle of Uganda Waragi and still make more than they would if they sold to the distillery; also, there was little enforcement of the prohibitions against the sale of raw enguli directly to consumers. By 1989, the central distillery was no longer buying from local producers, opting instead to use industrially produced sugarcane distillates.

Questions of temperance and treasury remain important in Uganda today. There is little doubt that part of the state's interest in more tightly regulating the sale and production of alcohol stems from their interest in capturing the 172,000,000 USD lost each year to the "fiscal leakage" of untaxed informal production (Euromonitor Consulting 2016). In this aim, the government is joined by lobbyists working across sub-Saharan Africa on behalf of the multinational drinks industry who would very much like to capture a larger share of the market by forcing people currently drinking informally produced alcoholic beverages to shift to their bottled beers and spirits (Bakke and Endal 2010).

Indeed, the lack of interest in the problem of alcohol in the early 2000s, discussed in the introduction, was something of an outlier, with the regulation of the production and sale of alcohol again becoming a matter of heated debate during the years we were conducting the research that informs this book. This debate was complicated by the range of stakeholders involved, with the Ministry of Health and the Ministry of Trade, Industry, and Cooperatives on the one hand, and the multinational alcohol industry and civil society organizations on the other, squaring off. While measures were proposed, and even passed by some local governments that would restrict drinking hours and regulate the sale of alcohol to minors, the majority of the debate centered on the production and sale of the small cheap plastic sachets of waragi known as tot packs. Concerns over tot packs and informally distilled waragi were not simply related to their popularity among heavy drinkers. Rather, these concerns focused on the accessibility of this form of alcohol to schoolchildren—because of its low cost and the ease with which it can be concealed in a pocket or school bag (Edyegu 2009)—and on the frequency with which the methylated spirits that sometimes found their way into the tot packs were resulting in death and blindness (Okungu 2010; Ahimbisibwe 2010; Anguyo and Masaba 2012). Bills aimed at developing national alcohol policies were proposed in 2009 and 2016, but battles between the ministry of trade and the ministry of health prevented them from becoming law. In 2019, Uganda passed the National Alcohol Control Policy.[3] This policy banned the tot packs and restricted the hours that bars could be opened. While the ban on tot packs has effectively removed them from the market, people have shifted toward unpackaged, informally produced enguli, which producers pour from jerry cans directly into bottles brought by their customers.

GOING OUT

In Uganda today, bars are crucial sites of sociality. It might even be possible to say that they are the primary form of public space. While one might chat briefly with friends at the market or on the cement veranda of a small shop, bars are virtually the only place a person can go for any kind of leisure or sustained social interaction outside of the house, workplace, or religious institutions. Given that the world of the house and compound is largely dominated by women and children, bars are especially important places for men, a fact essential for understanding the specific challenges faced by men who decide to stop drinking.

One would be hard-pressed to find tonto for sale in a bar today. While tonto can be found for sale in some villages, in the city its role is largely limited to its place as one of the few required items found among the bride-wealth offerings brought by the groom's family to the bride's during the increasingly elaborate *kwanjula* ceremony. Its rarity is not due to a complete urban rejection of traditional drinks. Rather it is the extreme scarcity of the specific varieties of bananas, primarily *kisubi* and *kayinja* (*musa*), that are used to produce it, most of which have been attacked by banana wilt. While some brewers are experimenting with adding sugars and other types of genetically modified bananas, it remains a comparatively expensive beverage.

By contrast, the freshly brewed grain beers historically drunk in the eastern and northern regions of the country are readily available in many outlying neighborhoods in Kampala. Located off the main roads, behind the other stalls and shops, one can find groups of people drinking *malwa*, warm and thick with millet, out of communal clay pots through long straws made of dried reeds. The bars smell faintly of dried millet and urine, as there are no toilets. Shaded by a tarp or a small, thatched hut, seated on wooden benches, the drinkers are served by the woman who is both the brewer and seller of the drink. These drinkers are usually older people, at least in middle age, and mostly Bateso, Acholi, and Luo. Together they can meet at these bars to talk and enjoy recordings of traditional music played loudly on the speakers. Some *malwa* bars are organized around more formal drinking clubs, and larger *malwa* bars may be divided into named sections, often named for the English premier league teams, where different groups of drinkers sit with their pots on a regular basis.

Closer to the road one finds small bars in blocks of one-room *muzigo* apartments that share an outdoor toilet and bathing area with the apartments themselves. These bars are usually managed by a single woman and "the girl," an attractive young woman who will have been hired to serve the drinkers and attract them to the bar. The drinks include bottled beer, plastic tot packs of waragi, and sodas served from a small refrigerator. These small bars might also sell any number of domestically produced drinks. These might include tonto, *kwete* or *umkomboti* (brewed from maize), *kaliga* (brewed from yeast and sugar), and *omunanasi* (brewed from pineapples, tea, and ginger). These bars might also have enguli or crude waragi available for purchase. There are usually two or three plastic chairs for seating, and a TV and DVD player might be placed in a corner, with Ugandan music videos playing most of the time. A small foam mattress and blanket, the bed for the girl, are rolled up and hidden in the corner, to be taken out and unrolled once the bar closes. The customers, almost exclusively men—*boda boda* drivers taking a break, small-time land brokers arranging a sale—usually come alone. They come for the drinks, but mostly they come to see the girl, hoping that they might finally get a chance with her. If the girl leaves the bar to return home or work somewhere else, they will stop coming and find another place to drink. Everyone wants to buy for her in hopes of winning her favor. This she may use to her advantage, allowing the men to pay for her beer and then drinking from a beer bottle that she has refilled with water in advance, allowing her to keep the money the men have spent on the beer for herself. This additional income is crucial as these girls might only be paid 50,000 UGX a month, plus meals and "lodging" in the form of that thin rolled-up mattress in the corner.

Slightly larger bars have more amenities. Besides the chairs and the TV, there might be sofas, a pool table, or even a jukebox. A much larger refrigerator will be filled with a larger selection of bottled beers and sodas, and there will also be bottles and tot packs of formally distilled waragi for sale. There may even be a few rooms for people to stay the night. Since they are more spacious, patrons can easily move the chairs around, sometimes carrying them outside, to sit wherever they wish. Most of the people who come to these bars are men. They also have more customers, making them important places for the forms of movement and sociality discussed later in the chapter. Some might come alone, but such bars also serve as meeting points for groups of friends, coworkers, and local government officials. A few women might also come, in hopes that someone will buy for them, but these women are largely taken to be people with serious drinking problems, and they are rarely successful in their requests for free drinks. The women who own these bars also serve as counselors and confidantes to men who have come to the bar seeking solace and advice when they are having trouble at work or at home with their partners.

Closer to the center of town and near the universities, one finds bigger bars. These enormous and sometimes elaborately decorated spaces are typically quiet until late at night, their customers still at work or preferring to start their night at the smaller, cheaper bars on the back streets. Along the suburban highways there are also large bars and pork joints, some with occasional concerts and elaborate thatched shades overlooking the lake.

The colonial signification of bottled lager-style beer, as the drink of the modern wage laborer, has remained true across all of these spaces and is incessantly pointed out on billboards and other advertisements for beer. This is especially true of the higher-end brands like SABMiller's subsidiary company Nile Breweries Limited's flagship brand, Nile Special, whose enormous billboards featuring slogans like "The True Reward of Progress" cover the pedestrian bridges spanning Uganda's main highways. In 2015, an especially memorable Nile Special campaign featured a lineup of male workers, each in distinctive attire—a judge in a curly white wig and robe, a construction worker in a hard hat, a businessman in a suit. Above the men, the billboard proclaimed, "Here's to the men who do an honest hard day's work. . . . We salute you. You've Earned It." The association between wage earning and beer drinking is also true of entry level brands, like Nile Breweries' Eagle, brewed from local sorghum, sold for approximately half the price of a Nile Special, and targeted at people who might be lured away from cheaper locally brewed drinks like *malwa* and *umkomboti*. Eagle's ads replicate the lessons about the relationship between beer, time, work-discipline, and industrial capitalism (Thompson 1967) found in Miller's iconic American slogan "It's Miller Time." In Uganda, the ads for Eagle depict wage-laboring construction workers, hard hats prominently positioned on the table, pointing to their watches (which read 3:59 p.m.) and toasting their day's work as an eagle soars over a sunset (which is occurring three hours early), all emblazoned with the slogan "*Saawa ya Eagle*" (It's Eagle time). Bell, humorously said to be favored by grandmothers given its low ABV, won favor in China with its 2007 ad campaign, which promised that "Bell evenings are followed by clear mornings"; these words were sung to an energizing pop melody played over a video showing middle-class news broadcasters enjoying a drink together at night and getting up to produce the early morning program the next day without a hangover.

In the final years of this project, this pictorial discourse around bottled beer and modern middle-class identity was taken in a new direction with ads for Club and Nile Gold that featured images of young cosmopolitan women and slogans that pointed to the originality and superior taste of the beers in question. The

Black Bell billboard depicted a young man dressed in red sneakers abstractly fly-ing through a cloud of golden dust. Its slogan promised consumers the chance to "Go Full Flavor, Go Next Level," inviting well-educated young people to try some-thing new and to further distinguish themselves (Bourdieu 1984) from their par-ents and from drinkers of the now commonly available brands.[4]

Waragi and enguli also remain popular. At bigger bars, one might find drinkers buying bottles of nationally branded Uganda Waragi, but the hotly contested tot packs were more common during the period of our research. These were certainly drunk in bars, but they could also be bought at nearly any shop, supermarket, mar-ket, or even from roadside sellers. As noted above, these tot packs are small and cheap and could easily be slipped into the pocket of a jacket, to be taken later or on the go, a practice said to be common among *boda boda* motorcycle taxi drivers as they pass the time waiting at their stages for customers. Enguli is available for sale in both urban and rural areas. It can be bought by the bottle (usually a 350ml Fanta bottle) in small bars or from the homes of a small number of older women who are known to keep a 5L jerry can of enguli for sale. These older women sell mostly to men, or to the children who are sent to buy for them.

WOMEN

Women are not expected to drink in the way that men are, but women in Uganda do drink on occasion, and in some cases drink quite heavily. That said, women's relationship to alcohol, and more specifically to the social institution of the bar, is complicated. Unmarried women and girls are admonished by their families to avoid bars, and married women are advised only to visit them with their hus-bands' consent. While men do bring women to bars to demonstrate their prestige, or look for women in bars who they might be able to buy for and thus secure as a sexual partner, to go to a bar in hopes of meeting a man who might buy for her puts a woman in a potentially dangerous situation. Women who frequent bars are stigmatized due to the assumption that their drinking is made possible by their willingness to have sex with men who will buy for them. Mockingly called *malaya* (prostitute), *gaali ekozeeko* (used bicycle), and "football"—that is, kicked by whoever finds it—women in bars face a series of reputational risks that men do not. Women are also at real risk of being raped or killed if they pass out before reaching home (Wolff et al. 2006). For all these reasons, it is more common for women to drink at home or at large family celebrations where they can feel free to enjoy themselves.

That said, there are some women, especially female university students, who do go out to bars more frequently, often hopping between multiple bars in the same night in hopes of finding men with resources, jokingly referred to as "spon-sors" in current slang, for a night or for a lifetime. Women looking for men might also pose as bar attendants, taking men's money and buying their drinks for them at the counter, in hopes of striking up a financially beneficial relationship. They also go simply to have fun. During her student days at Makerere, Sarah often went out in the company of friends. Heading for a bar or a house party where at least one person in the group has a personal connection—"my friend's friend's boyfriend has a bar where we can go"—they would rely on the links of an interpersonal chain of trust for some measure of security and confidence that there would be someone to help them if things were to go wrong. One of the women would also avoid drinking until they got home, serving as the security for the rest, making sure they got home all right. While women often buy the first round of drinks themselves, when they go out to a bar there is also a hope that one of them will meet a man, usually an older man, who will buy not only for her, but for the whole group of friends. The aim of hooking a man who will make such purchases is less to actually drink the drinks in the bar than it is to secure alcohol and cash that can be taken home and shared in the privacy and comfort of their own rooms. Being savvy university women, they might engage two men in this way at the same time, with one being instructed to fund a "standing order" by giving a lump sum of money to the bar attendant and the other ordering drinks for the women as they need them. While both men think they are the one purchasing the drinks the women are holding, the women collect the money given for the "standing order" from the bar attendant as they head for home. Alternatively, they might order two beers at once, one cold and one warm. Since only one of these beers will be opened at the bar, they can easily carry the second home with them.[5] Women employed in sales might also visit bars with possible clients in the hopes of closing business deals. When Sarah was working in a corporate sales job, men who had failed to give her business during the day could be lured to the bar after work. There, as they thought they were in the process of poaching her, she could get them to break a business deal while drunk.

This said, outside of the narrow range of contexts where women can drink with minimal reputational risk, women who frequent bars endure a great deal of physical and emotional pain, and this can lead them to drinking even more as a way of numbing this pain. Safe in their homes and beds, they might drink what they have brought home from the bar or what they have stocked in their "minibars" of tot packs and bottles of waragi stashed secretly and out of sight. The stigma of drinking can also make it more difficult for women to seek treatment. The experience of being ostracized by their families and by society as a whole can lead them to retreat further into isolation or into the small bars where they have been able to find a measure of friendship and acceptance. When they do seek treatment in formal rehabilitation centers, they are further stigmatized by the men in those centers. They are treated as if their lives are wasted, unrecoverable, and their stories are treated as gossip. Women who are also celebrities have even more to fear as their admissions to rehabilitation centers are hot topics for tabloid journalists.

OGULA OMWENGE?

At the bar, it is not only the drinking, but also the experience of spending, that is the pleasure. People buy for themselves, and they buy for each other, setting aside the tensions and pressures of economizing that rule in everyday life. *Malwa* pots are refilled, bottles of waragi are shared, and rounds of beer are bought for the table, or even for the whole bar. In contemporary Luganda slang, to go out on the town is signified by the phrase *kulya kaasi*, to eat cash.[6] When one finally has a job or otherwise finds themselves with money, they might go out drinking "to wash off the dust of poverty." As this phrase indicates, treating oneself and one's friends to a drink is especially important in moments of transition out of difficulty. In a world where money is usually carefully budgeted, resources painstakingly conserved, the bar provides a unique site for the enjoyment and enactment of indulgence and unchecked generosity. As the anthropologist Gregor Dobler writes about Namibia, bars enable "self-assertion in the context of economic deprivation," providing "one of the few experiences of detachment from the plight of everyday life" (2010, 188). While an analysis of consumption might have us focus on the pleasures people take in the items consumed, the Ugandan bar helps us to focus on the pleasure of spending itself, the bar providing a moment of relief from the ever-pressing need to economize.

While one might enjoy the occasional drink purchased by another and might very much hope to be in a bar when someone with means is buying for the table or even for the whole bar,[7] the ability to buy for oneself and for others constitutes an important marker of status. Sarah fondly remembers having thrown a party on her twenty-first birthday at which she spent more than one month's salary buying crates of beer and large quantities of roasted meat for her workmates. They danced the night away, and Sarah basked in her newfound esteem. Some of the friendships that were started that night are still important sources of support and joy in her life. Indeed, the status marker of being able to purchase alcohol for others is so widely understood that when children refuse to do something for their parents, their parents might ask the rhetorical question "*Ogula omwenge?*" (Do you buy alcohol?). While this question might seem like a strange one to ask of a child who has just refused to help with the laundry, it is intended in the same way that an American parent might ask "Who do you think you are?" of a child who has similarly refused to bow to their authority. In the question "*Ogula omwenge?*" and in the negative answer that is sure to follow, the parent both asks the child to reflect on their relative unimportance and reveals the reach of this way of reckoning social status. Indeed, the much-mocked figure of the *kanywa mugule* is ridiculed precisely because he asks others to buy for him, the name literally meaning "Buy and give it to me."

While there are no doubt questions of status tied up with buying, we also want to highlight the pleasures and forms of relief tied up in the spending itself and the ways that these pleasures are connected with larger dynamics of tension and flow. While money certainly does allow alcohol to flow, it is also the alcohol itself that makes the pleasurable flow of money possible. As the iconic *kadongo kamu* musician Paul Kafeero put it in his song "*Dipo Nazigala*" (I closed the depot), in which he sang about his own efforts to stop drinking, "The one on the head buys the next bottle," highlighting how the effects of alcohol loosen one's purse strings. While the effects of alcohol might lead one to forget one's problems, the spending itself is also a form of relief from the ever-present need to worry over money. Importantly, while the pleasure of spending was at one point limited by what one had in one's pocket and what the barkeeper was willing to sell on credit, mobile money apps have now made it possible for a person to drink through a more substantial portion of their savings.

PULEESA, STRESS, AND TENSION

The strain from which one might seek relief in the bar most often takes the form of mounting demands and misfortunes. In both city and village, people refer to this feeling with the English cognate *puleesa* (pressure). In the city, this feeling may also be referred to with the English word "stress," whether the conversation is occurring in English or Luganda. This is the feeling of the press of demands, usually for money. It may come when you have gone to collect a child from school who has been chased home for lack of fees and while you are there, you get a call from the school of another child threatening to do the same, all the while thinking that your landlord may soon be coming to evict you. "*Oh, nina puleesa*" (I have a lot of pressure on me). Your boss at work may be demanding many things from you. Or the bank is calling you about the loan you've failed to pay back. While this experience of pressure and stress is often caused by a lack of money, people sometimes seek relief from it by letting the last of what is in their pocket enter the flow of the bar. Men escape from pressure, escape the air of the house and compound, dense with women and the ever-present reminders of their unmet responsibilities to them, escape the office boss and his constant demands, escape the pressures of upcoming exams, to the friendship and flow of the bar.

Poverty and inequality clearly play major roles as sources of these forms of pressure. Understanding the historical roots of the economic problems that shape life in contemporary Uganda requires understanding the impact of many historical factors including the precolonial trade in both slaves and ivory, the cash crop export economy imposed during the colonial period by the British, the destruction of this fragile and highly unequal economy by the governments of Milton Obote and Idi Amin, and the economic impacts of neoliberalism as it has been embraced by Museveni's government (Mutibwa 1992; Reid 2017; Brett 1972; Greco, Martiniello, and Wiegratz 2018). While a full review of this history is beyond the scope of this book, it is important for readers to understand that the economic difficulties experienced by those whose stories we tell in this book are part of much larger historical processes and not of their own making.

Given the limited opportunities for formal employment in the public and private sectors, many of Kampala's residents support themselves and their families through work in the informal economy. They drive *boda boda* motorcycle taxis, hawk used clothes, sell snacks, and work other petty jobs. While these informal microenterprises may have been heralded by neoliberal development organizations in the 2000s (Mallaby 2004; Elyachar 2005; Scherz 2014), the establishment of the Kampala Capital City Authority (KCCA) in 2010 put these informal vendors at risk. Seeking to transform a city "littered with vendors," the KCCA enforcement officers arrested and impounded their wares in the name of order and cleanliness (Doherty 2021). This situation has compounded the precarity of Kampala's youth by further narrowing the available options for securing a livelihood and amplifying the *pulessa* and stress of everyday life.

Tension is something quite different. As opposed to the pressure and stress created by a series of mounting and all too certain demands, tension is the feeling of facing an uncertain future. It is the feeling of waiting for news about a job application. Waiting for an upcoming visa interview. Waiting to know the results of a medical test. Where stress and pressure might call for a night of distraction and forgetting, tension suspends. The appetite is gone. Music is annoying. You want to be alone and wait it out in silence, with your goosebumps (*olutiko*) and racing heart. The moment for the bar is after, once the news, good or bad, has come; the bar is what draws a line between the suspended time of tension and the life that still lies ahead.

The situation during the 2016 Ugandan general election was tense. The Democratic Alliance (TDA) campaign slogan *"Omusajja agenda"* (The man is leaving) spoke of the TDA's determination to see the NRM government, which had been in power since 1986, finally go. In response to these ambitions, government security forces marched through the streets of Kampala armed with AK-47 rifles, claiming to protect traders from would-be rioters. At the same time, foreign companies were said to be taking their capital out of the country, and many Ugandans with means and families abroad left for short-term work or holidays.

While there was less concern about violence in regard to the district, subcounty, and parliamentary elections taking place during the same month, the outcomes of these elections were also less certain, and they likewise generated a great deal of effort and anxious waiting. This state of anticipation was shared by one of this book's coauthors. In February 2016, George campaigned for a second time for a post as a district councillor, which would allow him to represent his town council to the district. George and his team campaigned hard, pinning up posters and hiring a truck with a loudspeaker to broadcast his campaign speeches. Many supporters promised to vote for him, and it seemed possible that he could win.

During the time of vote counting on election day, he was "on tension" awaiting the results. His heart panicked as he worried about receiving bad news. He worried about the money he had invested in the campaign. He worried that he might come to know what people really thought about him. He decided to leave the counting place until the votes were tallied. He bought a bottle of water and went to the home of Sarah's mother, a longtime friend and confidante. He told her that he wanted to sleep while he waited for the votes. She sympathized with him and gave him a mat to lie on in her sitting room. She even gave him a radio and advised him to listen to results from other places. He only told one person on his campaign team where he had gone and asked the man to come for him if he emerged as the winner. He switched off his phone. The water helped a little bit, but the radio did not; he heard but never listened to any of what they said.

Thinking after a while that the counting might be done, he reluctantly switched on the phone. His heart was beating so hard that if there had been anyone near him, they could have heard it beating. He was glad that Sarah's mom had gone away to feed her animals. After twenty minutes, he didn't hear his phone ringing. He checked the signal, and it was on. He wondered, "What might have happened? Is it that everyone fears to call to tell me the bad news?" He tried to call the person at the tally center, and he didn't pick up. This was a bad sign. The man at the tally center eventually picked up the phone and told him, "George, the results from other stations have not yet come to me." George asked, "What about where you are? How has it been?" The man said "Here, the other man has beaten us. But don't worry; we may beat him double in the other voting areas." George called another man from a very rural place and the man said, "We have been beaten. But I am sure that we shall replace them at the center!" The man had not heard what had happened at the center. George knew he had lost.

Wanting to put the tension behind him, George called his *boda boda* driver to come for him. Reaching the bar where he had always held meetings with his friends, people cheered and told him, "You are our hero, despite the results." Then each one asked the bar lady to give him a bottle. Eventually, it felt like they were the winners. The owner of the bar put on high music and asked George to dance. He did because he felt good, knowing that he had done all he could. He called his mother and when she heard his happy voice, a heavy burden was lifted from her; she had been so worried about how he might feel if he lost. He felt like a free man, released from the tension that had held him in a state of paralysis as he lay on the floor of Sarah's mother's house waiting for the results.

The tension, the anxious state of suspended action, began to break as soon as George knew he had been defeated. But it was the cheering crowd at the bar, the alcohol itself, the music, and the encouragement to dance that allowed for his reentry into the normal flow of movement and connectivity. While George's story represents a major moment of his life, the role of the bar as a space for relieving paralyzing states of tension through the flow of alcohol and money occurs in more mundane ways as well. As people sit with the tensions of uncertain futures and the pressures of landlords knocking at the door demanding rent, the bar provides a space apart where those worries recede from view.

MOVEMENT

The movement found in the release from states of suspense and tension is joined by a second kind of movement that is perhaps even more central to the role that bars play for people in Uganda, and especially for men. This is the way that bars figure as spaces for movement, possibility, and the generation of new ideas and opportunities. Like the tactics of those involved in the opportunistic *kukiya-kiya* (zig-zag) economy in Zimbabwe, economic life in Uganda depends on constant movement (Jones 2010). As Jeremy Jones writes of Zimbabwe, "There is no guarantee of finding money in a given time and place . . . [and] this in turn requires movement. . . . [T]he more a person moves around, the more opportunities he/she encounters, the more people he/she meets, and the wider his/her network grows" (292). While many of the *kukiya-kiya* activities Jones describes involve more of a "setting aside" (294) of rules than those activities we are interested in here, his point about the necessity of movement and the value placed on mobility itself (cf. Melly 2017) is what resonates with so much of what we have heard from Ugandan men about the necessity of getting out of the house and putting oneself in the path of opportunity.

Bars not only figure as spaces where one can conjure plans with friends or come to feel like a winner in the face of defeat; they also serve as concrete sites for creating other forms of movement and belonging. This was certainly true of the small roadside bar called Kafene where we spent many long afternoons and evenings over the course of this project. Kafene lies on the edge of the Kampala-Entebbe highway, in what was a village and is now a rapidly gentrifying suburb. While the tiled bottled-beer bar and pork joint is primarily frequented by middle-class commuters and *matatu* drivers, who park their cars and *matatus* at the roadside as they stop to enjoy the expertly prepared banana leaf-bound bundles of brothy pork *luwombo*, the most regular customers are casual laborers working in construction and brickmaking for the posh new bungalows that increasingly cover the hillsides south of Kampala.

The outdoor seating area is calm and shaded by mango and jackfruit trees. Under the trees are a pair of rough wooden benches fixed together in the corner to make a long L, along with white plastic chairs and tables that can be moved and arranged as needed. Two one-room bars open onto this packed dirt patio. The first sells bottled beer and tot packs and bottles of waragi. The women who sell from this bar circulate among the drinkers on the patio and in the pork joint taking orders for drinks. When addressing the customers they drop back on their heels so that their knees nearly touch the floor in the traditional gesture of respect.

The other bar is furnished with low tables and low wooden armchairs with wide, sloping backs. To one side of the room are shelves and cabinets with containers of different locally made drinks. While the *umkomboti* drinkers often bring their liter-size yellow jerry cans out to the tables under the trees to sip the thick contents through plastic straws, at night the small enclosed *umkomboti* bar also fills with younger men and women, bathed in the green light of overhead bulbs and enjoying the music played loud on the speakers in the adjacent beer bar.

But now it is still afternoon, a beautiful sunny Saturday afternoon in mid-March 2018, and George is stopping by for a visit. George used to come here with his wife Agnes years ago to eat pork before they married, when she was still teaching at a nearby nursery school. Now living in a different part of town, he hadn't returned in years, but as we began this project in 2015, he began visiting again on a regular basis with the hope that Kafene might help us to think about the place of alcohol in Ugandan life.

The open window of the pork butchery is filled with big pieces of freshly slaughtered meat hanging on thick metal wires. There is also some being roasted, mostly hooves and ears, and the place is filled by the strong smell of roasting meat. Two women are busily tying *luwombo* while another is preparing a fire for their steaming. Cars and trucks are packed together by the roadside, their owners stopping in to grab roasted, fried, or fresh pork to take home with them.

There are men seated around a table sipping Ngule beer and a few taking *umkomboti*. Among them is Willy Ssali, whom George has come to know well over the years since we started the project, and George easily takes a seat next to him. Despite George's protests, Ssali flips open his small black flip phone to make a few quick calls to let his friends Sam Ddamba and Phillip Kayongo know that George has arrived. These three men sit with each other at Kafene nearly every day. Ssali was born and grew up in this village, and Ddamba and Kayongo came from villages in Masaka in search of work in the 1990s.

Bricklaying was their primary employment, but since the village is near the shores of Lake Victoria, they also learned to fish. It was in fishing where they made the money that allowed Ddamba and Kayongo to buy their plots of land. Ssali did not need to buy land because his family already owned a big *kibanja* on which they have a family graveyard, and Ssali was allocated a part of the *kibanja* for himself and his growing family.

Ssali, the most talkative of the trio, says that by the time his friends came to stay, the area was a typical village, with thick forests and swamps. They fetched water from wells. There were wild animals that destroyed the food in their gardens. The population of the area was low, and each family knew each other, supporting one another in times of both sorrow and happiness. Many families had graveyards around the village because they had long held large plots of land. Ssali recalls being frightened by the darkness at night as a child as he passed through forests and banana plantations.

Now, twenty years later, the area has drastically changed. Given the village's proximity to both the capital and the airport, it is considered an area of prime land, and many people have come to settle in this place that was once a village. Ssali says that a day cannot pass without land being bought in the area. Those who buy are mainly government or NGO workers willing to pay any price. "They never bargain because they have the money to spend," says Ssali.

In the past, this land was mostly used for subsistence and commercial farming. Now it is mostly residential, with huge bungalows lining the road. The dirt roads are rutted from the posh cars moving to and from the main road. Some of the new houses are imposing two- or even three-story mansions. At the same time, the small older houses remain alongside, inhabited by their original owners, even as those owners have sold parts of their plots to the new people in the area. There are also landowners who refuse to sell, mainly because they do not want to part with their family's land. Because of this, it is not uncommon to find a garden of beans neighboring a three-story house.

All of this new construction has also created jobs for builders and providers of local building materials, including Ddamba, Ssali, and Kayongo. Bricks are in high demand and every morning site owners or their brokers are out looking for bricks to buy or people to hire who can make them on-site. These three friends now make bricks to sell to the new landowners to earn a living. Each of them can make bricks individually, but most times they are hired as a group to make them at the site. They dig and pile the earth, then mix it with water and soften it using their feet. Then they heap the soil into a mound and leave it for a week or two to cure. Then they mix it again with water and put the wet soil in wooden molds of their desired size. They all say that the most difficult part is firing the bricks in a furnace. This has to be heated with firewood, which, due to increasing population pressure and the production of bricks like these, is becoming less available.

For brickmakers like Willy Ssali and his friends, Kafene provides a crucial site for connecting with people who might hire them. As Ddamba put it, "Drinking helps me to get useful friends and job opportunities, which I wouldn't get if I was a *mulokole* [born-again Christian] who sat at home. . . . One day I came here to pass time. I had not worked on that day and decided to have a walk. As soon as I reached here, my friends told me of a house that needed a new roof. We negotiated about the payment, and I earned 150,000 UGX. I had come here just to pass time but went back with that money."

Bars also figured as sites for business opportunities for those not involved in manual labor. Mark Ssekandi is a corporate lawyer who was a patient at the exclusive Lakeview rehabilitation center, discussed in the following chapter. He was the son of one of the first Ugandans allowed to join the all-white Kampala Club in the last days of the British protectorate and now, being himself a member of that private club, conducted his business of helping entrepreneurs formalize and register their enterprises from a seat beneath the shade of a tree in the club's lush gardens or from the back of a passenger van that he had outfitted "like a board-room" and which he parked on the club's premises.

For all of their differences, these men all saw bars as putting them in the pathway of opportunity and removing them from the dangerous stagnation of the house. While proverbs like "the one who does not settle down never gets chance to eat a miser's chicken," and "the one with two homes dies of hunger" warn drinkers against spending so much time loitering in bars, men are also admonished to get out of the house so that opportunity might find them, and often the only place to go is the bar. There are many Luganda sayings that work along these lines. "Avoid sitting in one place." "A free goat feeds better than one on the rope." "The one who does not travel thinks that his mother is the best cook." "An opportunity is like the wind"—meaning that it blows through quickly, so you must be prepared and in the right place at the right time. These proverbs speak to the value placed on movement, experience, traveling, and putting yourself in the pathway of opportunity more generally. While bars may sometimes be spaces of excessive loitering, they also figure as precisely the kinds of places where such opportunities might be found. While we might think of drinkers, and especially daytime drinkers, as retreating from work and movement, here the potential for connection and conversation allows for the real or imagined possibility of work and forward momentum.

FRIENDSHIP

Bars like Kafene are also central sites for building and maintaining friendships between men. While they work together, Willy Ssali, Sam Ddamba, and Phillip Kayongo drink with each other at Kafene nearly every day. Whether or not they have money to spend, they know that they can come and either buy for others or let others buy for them—trading rounds not just in a night, but over months and years. As they sit, they exchange ideas about work, politics, and women. They swap stories of funny things that happened to them in the past. And they come together to support one another both emotionally and financially in times of celebration and sorrow.

While this is particularly true among men, the bar also serves as an important site for care and friendship among women, and particularly for those women who feel excluded from more typical sites of female friendship. Glenda, a woman whom we followed over the course of a long series of engagements with inpatient rehabil-itation programs, lived for years in the cramped one-room bar of a woman named Deborah. Marginalized by the prosperous relatives who raised her after her par-ents died, Glenda found a home in this bar and a true friend in Deborah. Deborah looked after her in the ghetto, stayed with her in the hospital as she lay in danger of dying from tuberculosis, and visited her regularly while she sought inpatient treatment in the drug and alcohol unit at the national psychiatric hospital.

In the following chapter, you will hear these friendships trivialized as people are encouraged to avoid their former "partners in crime," to change their "people and places." While spending time in bars might indeed prove difficult for some, we do want to highlight the implicit assumptions that little of worth will be lost in this transition and that there will surely be other places where the ex-drinker can go to rebuild a different set of social connections. Thinking about bars not only as spaces of recreation, but as sites for opportunity and for building of productive connections and deep friendships, helps us to understand why the advice to avoid bars and old friends might be quite worrisome.

In Uganda, one cannot simply pick up and start over again. Finding a home, a job, or even someone trustworthy enough to repair one's car fundamentally depends on being positioned within a dense web of trusting relationships. While relationships forged in bars, like all relationships, are not universally positive, they are indeed relationships and cannot be severed without cost. These relations and the forms of mobility they enable are put at risk when someone decides to stop drinking. With this in mind, we ask how and in what ways the therapeutic pathways explored in the chapters that follow address this situation. Do they allow for the continuity of old friendships on new terms, or do they demand a complete cessation of these relationships? Do they create opportunities for the creation of new ties, and if so through what means? If we know that well-being in Uganda, and perhaps everywhere, depends on connection and that bars are the primary public spaces in Uganda where connection occurs, especially for men, what happens when the life sustained in the bar becomes one's undoing? What happens when one must turn away from this singular space of sociality, movement, and trust?

2

Once an Addict . . .

Learning the Chronic Relapsing Brain Disease Model in Kampala's Rehabilitation Centers

MAURICE

On a hot dry afternoon in January 2018, George and Sarah met at a taxi stage in central Kampala to walk to meet Maurice, a friend of Sarah's, who was currently staying in the ghetto near the university. Sarah had known Maurice for many years already. She had seen him move in and out of rehabilitation centers four times. Maurice's parents had been well off when he was a child, but his dad was a heavy drinker. When his dad learned he had HIV, his drinking only increased, and he spent most of the family's money on alcohol before he died. His mother died of AIDS four years later. Maurice's paternal uncle in Kampala took him in and raised him. These same relatives had now paid out of pocket for several of his stays in rehab. After his last stay, he had returned home and while looking for a novel found a stack of ten US one-hundred-dollar bills: his uncle's wife was saving for a back operation and had hidden her savings within the pages of the book. He took one of the bills and went out to drink. This was before Sarah started working on this project, but Sarah had been with his family when they took him to Luzira Prison to keep him away from alcohol, at least for a little while. He had now been out of prison for five months, living in the ghetto again and drinking even more than before.

Sloping down from the main road, behind the big bars and pork joints, George and Sarah began to snake through the narrow roads lined with mud and wattle houses and sewage trenches, the road so narrow that the iron sheet roofs of the houses opposite one another nearly touched in the center, making a tunnel. Three women in their early twenties were washing clothes in wide plastic basins. A little further down, other women stood outside of a small grocery shop, cooking food in enormous saucepans to sell. Music blared from a nearby video rental shop and people shouted to be heard. The air was sharp with the smell of alcohol and stale urine, and George felt nervous as people stared at them critically.

After a while, they found Maurice sitting on a wooden bench on the veranda of a small shop with some other men filling out football betting forms. Seeing Sarah, Maurice jumped up and hugged her. Maurice is in his early thirties, tall and strongly built. He had boils all over his body and wounds on his face, elbow, and leg. As he talked, his words slid together. "Sarah, buy me a drink." Sarah offered instead to buy him some food and left to go find the women with the saucepans.

When Sarah returned, Maurice picked lazily at his plate of *matooke* and fish stew. As he ate, Sarah asked how things were going with his recovery. "I don't have much to tell," he said. "I don't want to stop. Maybe reducing."

"How much are you taking now?" George asked.

"Buy me one so I can show you."

George was beginning to feel that this visit had been a waste.

Maurice went on talking to Sarah, jokingly referring to George as her husband, asking her if George could help him to realize his dream of studying in Russia, asking an old man nearby to buy him a drink. The old man did not respond.

. . .

Maurice had relapsed, and Sarah was trying to bring him back to the AA meetings they had once attended together. This way of thinking about what was happening to Maurice, the meetings and the rehab centers Maurice had attended, and Sarah's hopes that he might attend again, were all part of an emergent assemblage (Ong and Collier 2005) of programs, ideas, and ways of living that defined problem drinking as a chronic relapsing brain disease (CRBD) that is both manageable and yet incurable. Building on earlier work that took place in Europe and America, a passionate group of Ugandan psychiatrists, priests, former drinkers, and others have built a small, but growing, network of inpatient rehabilitation programs and Alcoholics Anonymous (AA) fellowships in Kampala and in other towns around the country. Modeled on European and American addiction treatment programs, these rehabilitation centers have introduced new ways of understanding what problem drinking is, new ways of understanding the self in relation to such problems, and new forms of social connection and support.

In this chapter, we explore the workings of two of Uganda's most prominent rehabilitation centers, one public and one private, and the broader network of AA meetings and recovery organizations that are scattered across Kampala and other towns. Building on previous work in the anthropology of addiction (Garcia 2010; Hansen 2018), we argue that despite the constant exhortations to change, the models of time and the self that define the work of these spaces leave many people feeling trapped in an unchangeable condition. Further, and perhaps most importantly, these models place certain limits on the social relationships that people in recovery are able to build with one another and with their families. Given the importance of social connections in Uganda and the role that bars play in social life, these limits can have personal and practical consequences. While this way of thinking about addiction and "boundaries" is something many readers might take for granted, in the chapters that follow we explore three other models of problem drinking that provide different answers to these crucial questions of the self and the social.

REHAB

Maurice had passed through inpatient recovery programs many times before George and Sarah met him in 2018, and he would go on to stay in others again over the time that we knew him. Some of the "rehabs" in Uganda are small programs, privately owned and run out of small bungalows or storefronts by other people in recovery, but others are considerably larger. These centers are also linked to a handful of AA meetings that constitute an important part of the recovery landscape. These meetings serve people who have come through inpatient rehabilitation programs and also people who have been brought to the meetings directly by friends who were already attending. In addition to the treatment programs and AA groups, there are also several research and advocacy organizations doing research, policy analysis, and alcohol abuse prevention work with youth.

In this chapter, we focus on the two largest rehabilitation centers: the Alcohol and Drug Unit at Butabika Hospital[1] and Lakeview Recovery Center. While these centers differ from one another in several ways, they are both important points of origin and energy for the growing interest in addiction and recovery in Uganda. They also serve as the most likely points of first contact for families looking to explore what this relatively new mode of addressing drinking problems might have to offer.

Both of these programs can trace their beginnings to a moment in the early 1980s when several Catholic religious orders began to notice that some of their priests were struggling with problems with alcohol. A priest who had been introduced to AA for help with his own drinking by a group of missionaries and a man who that priest had in turn helped to stop drinking took the initiative to start an AA fellowship in a private home, and small numbers of priests and lay people began to come stay for a few days and attend AA meetings. There was no counseling or other medical support, but the meetings grew in popularity, and by 1992 bishops were formally sending priests to the fellowship for treatment. By 1998, there was a growing realization that the problems of alcohol in Uganda were bigger than this single fellowship could address and that there was a need for something larger and more formal. The four orders involved decided to invite a priest from the United States, running a hostel for people living with substance use disorders in Portland, Oregon, to come and talk about this work in Uganda.

Inspired by this visit, in 2001, a team including Dr. Basangwa, a psychiatrist and the executive director of Butabika Hospital, traveled to the United States for a six-month training program to acquire the expertise necessary to start Uganda's first inpatient treatment centers.

Butabika Hospital

Butabika Hospital was founded in 1955 by the British protectorate government in Uganda (Pringle 2019). Today, its sprawling compound still lies at the edge of the city, at the end of a taxi route that winds its way past houses and suburban trading centers and markets until it reaches a long road overlooking the lake that leads nowhere but here. Past the single roadside chapatti vendor and the security officers staffing the high arched gate is a spotlessly clean, carefully mowed compound of intersecting paths, lawns, and low brick buildings that serve as the wards. Some patients move freely about the paths dressed in loose fitting standard-issue green cotton uniforms: shorts and shirts for the men and dresses for the women. The patients in the acute ward are more restricted, and they shout at passersby from behind the high barbed-wire fence that surrounds their building.

The Alcohol and Drug Unit (ADU) was among the newest additions to the hospital. In 2003, Dr. Basangwa had become increasingly concerned about the prevalence of psychiatric problems related to alcohol and drug abuse on the wards and in Kampala more generally. He had already started a small outpatient clinic to address alcohol and drug addiction, but he also knew that there were patients whose primary problems were related to alcohol and drug use who were being admitted to the general wards and did not feel comfortable there. Having been interested in addressing problems related to addiction for some time, he was finally able to act by taking advantage of a moment of interest in expanding the hospital to propose a new ward that would be dedicated to serving people living with addictions to alcohol and other drugs. In 2006, the buildings were completed, and Sr. Nantambi, who is still the head nurse on the unit, traveled to East London for three months of training in addiction treatment.

Between 2015 and 2018, the ADU could hold twenty-eight men in the public ward and ten men and women in the private wing; women who could not afford to stay in a private room were also occasionally housed in other women's wards in the hospital. Both the public and private wards were nearly always full to capacity, with a lengthy waiting list. Patients staying in the public wing did not pay for treatment, while patients in the private wing paid approximately 80,000 UGX per day and were also sometimes accompanied by a family caretaker who was permitted to stay in their room with them.[2] These patients were all attended to by Sr. Nantambi, who was helped by a team of nurses, all women, dressed either in simple pink uniforms or in white dresses with wide red belts and neatly folded caps pinned to their hair. Also on hand was a psychiatric medical doctor who was primarily responsible for making the diagnoses and treatment plans.

Each of the patients is meant to stay for thirty to ninety days in the small block of sturdy brick buildings that lie behind an unlocked fence at the edge of the hospital. The buildings are set up around a neatly maintained grassy courtyard ringed with immature shrubs. There is also a canteen where patients can pay for meals when they tire of the standard fare.

Their days follow a standard routine which roughly corresponds to the Minnesota Model of addiction treatment common throughout the United States. There is breakfast, medication if needed, and then group educational sessions in the main hall until lunchtime. After lunch, patients have individual meetings with their therapists, watch television, or go out to play football and cricket. During the initial phases of detoxification, diazepam—a benzodiazepine also known as Valium—is used to treat the withdrawal symptoms. Other antipsychotics, antidepressants, and anticonvulsant drugs might also be used, depending on the situation. Patients are given vitamins and undergo blood tests for HIV, syphilis, liver function, and renal function. Former patients also come to lead an AA group on Saturday mornings.[3]

Lakeview Recovery Center

Lakeview is Butabika's private counterpart. Its seven-acre compound is perched on a hill several kilometers outside of Kampala, its multistoried dormitories and spacious administrative buildings overlooking an expansive view of the lush green hills beyond. While these buildings, completed in 2012, can now accommodate up to eighty clients at a time, Lakeview's first incarnation in 2001 could house only five. Demand soon overwhelmed the small space, and so the director looked to rent a bigger house that could accommodate more. First they found one that could accommodate twelve, and then one for eighteen, but there were still long waitlists. In 2009, they approached the Catholic archbishop of Kampala, and he gave them a lease on the land on which the center now stands.

Like Butabika, Lakeview's programming is modeled on American addiction treatment programs. The day is structured around individual meetings with personal counselors and a series of therapeutic activities, many of which take the form of formal classes. Bells ring to mark the time between one activity and the next. As at Butabika, most of these classes focus on teaching clients strategies for avoiding temptation and structuring their time after discharge, but there are also forays into other topics, such as the basics of Freudian psychology, foreign languages, and music. In addition, there are opportunities for exercise and community outreach work and for occupational therapy classes oriented toward teaching the skills necessary to move into new opportunities for microenterprises such as liquid soapmaking, charcoal briquette pressing, and indoor mushroom growing. Family members are invited to monthly "Family Saturdays," so that they can be educated about addiction and how to "manage" their relatives upon discharge. Medical care at Lakeview involves a self-assessment, a family assessment, a urinalysis drug screening, and a blood test looking at HIV status, Hepatitis B status, and liver and kidney function. The drugs used for detox vary according to the patient's ability to pay for them and often include diazepam, Neurontin, B12, appetite stimulants, and occasionally injections of the long-acting antipsychotic risperidone. Lakeview's executive director often emphasized that every aspect of their program has been carefully designed for maximum therapeutic benefit. This said, more often than not, a majority of the clients could be found playing chess, watching television, or hanging out talking with one another at "the beach," as the area designated for clothes washing was playfully nicknamed.

Lakeview's programs last substantially longer than those at Butabika, with clients staying at least 90 days for alcohol and 180 for other drugs or for multiple substances. Due to the high costs of this extended private program—a 90-day stay cost approximately 5.4M UGX (a little less than 2,000 USD or about as much as a year of university tuition)—their client population was typically about half of their eighty-person capacity.

MAURICE

In late February, George and Sarah returned to the ghetto to find Maurice and his friends sitting on the benches in front of the shop where they had met him before. Some of the men were drinking beer and sipping from plastic tot packs of waragi.

Maurice, to George and Sarah's surprise, wasn't drinking and looked surprisingly clean in his freshly washed striped t-shirt. He mustered the strength to stand, to welcome them and to hug Sarah, but his body trembled as they sat talking, his state of withdrawal showing itself on his body.

"Nothing is moving well. Everything is a mess. I wanted to resume attending AA. I am tired of drinking, and I can see the time running. I don't want to reach the middle of this year when I am still not sober, but I cannot become sober single handedly."

"What do you think is stopping you from doing this?" asked George.

"I stay and sleep here. You have seen these men. It is difficult to stay sober here. They offer me alcohol. I try to refuse, but when I feel stressed, it is hard to say no."

Sarah offered to give Maurice the number of another friend of theirs who coordinates the AA meetings and told him about an open meeting that was scheduled for the next day.

George asked Maurice where he was sleeping and how he manages to get money for food.

"I sleep here, where we are sitting. When it reaches 3:00 a.m., the shop owner allows me to sleep on this veranda. All of these guys do the same. I don't have money for food either, but if I wait until 11 at night the women selling food will give me the leftovers for free."

"Does your family know that you're here?" George asked.

"Yeah, but they don't come to see me here. Last week I went and found my mum at the office. We talked and talked. Before I left, she said, 'I know you want money, but the condition is one and you know it properly; you get sober and everything you want is available for you.' She gave me money for lunch and transport, and I came back here."

Another young man passed by and asked Maurice to share some of the food George and Sarah had bought for him. The man reminded Maurice that they were at university together. Maurice introduced the man to George and Sarah, saying that he is a tailor who comes here to drink whenever he gets money. Minutes later, Maurice asked his friend to leave, sending the rest of his food with him.

"I can't eat much because of the effects of the withdrawals. That's why I'm shivering."

Sarah asked, "How long have you been coming here?"

"Six years," he said.

"When you first came to Butabika, did you come from here?"

"Yes."

"How many times were you in the hospital?" asked George.

"I was at Butabika twice, and also two times in another rehab up country."

"Were your parents taking care to send you there?" George asked.

"My brother especially. Older than me. But when I went to see him two weeks ago, he told me, 'You know the deal, you sober up, we talk.' They can give me everything, a house, a car, but I know that I can't do this on my own. I need support. I have to cut myself off from these guys," he said, his eyes casting about to the men seated drinking nearby. "With them, there is no progress."

"Where do you think you will go?" Sarah asked.

"That's the reason why I don't leave them. I have nowhere to go. I tried going to the AA meeting the other day, but I got lost on the way."

CLASS

Like Maurice, who had once attended Makerere University, the vast majority of patients at both Lakeview and Butabika come from Uganda's English-speaking, university-educated upper and middle classes (Vorhölter 2017) and most had completed at least some university. The training sessions that punctuate the days in the rehabilitation centers replicate the rhythm, regularity, and didactic style of university classes. These classes are invariably held in English, and English is also the language of treatment and conversation among the patients and the families who come for visiting days and family education sessions. As in many contexts in Uganda, this choice to speak English is made in an effort to mark status. While the need to make a point about status makes a lot of sense in a potentially stigmatizing environment where the loss of face is at stake (Goffman 1959; 1986), it is also a linguistic choice that is only available to people who have secondary or even university-level educations. Patients at Butabika who could not speak fluently in English were marginalized, left out of most activities and conversations, and openly mocked. That said, such situations were relatively rare, for despite Butabika's program being public and requiring no payment, it still attracted a clientele who were exceptionally well-educated.

This class-stratified pattern of participation in inpatient rehabilitation programs is not only an outcome of pricing and referral structures but also reflects how "the addict" has been constructed as a figure of public concern in Uganda. While media attention to problems related to alcohol cuts across class, the form that this attention takes varies: stories about poor drinkers focus on the need to implement legislation to control the supply of alcohol and stories about elite drinkers focus on the need for medicalized intervention (see Netherland and Hansen 2016a). Celebrity testimonials figure prominently in this process of medicalization, allowing some members of the public to identify with unique patients heroically suffering and recovering from medical problems.

This form of publicity generally takes the form of feature-length newspaper and television stories of wealthy or otherwise prominent individuals who have suffered from addictions to alcohol and who are now living in recovery. In these stories, addiction appears as a condition afflicting singular individuals who are rhetorically presented as a possible mirror of the reader or an intimate other in the reader's life. That these stories center celebrities who are seen as successful is especially significant, as it negates the notion that alcohol abuse is the result of laziness, unemployment, or poverty and instead frames addiction as a disease capable of touching anyone. These stories also highlight the specter of squandered potential and the possibility for redemption, themes foundational to the recruitment of the male university students who constitute the majority of the patients presently enrolling in the rehabilitation centers and AA groups that we discuss in this chapter.

The public testimonial offered by Major General Pecos Kutesa in the inaugural episode of the award winning NTV series *Life Stories* is an example of this sort of publicity. Kutesa served as a celebrated field commander during the civil war that brought President Yoweri Museveni to power in 1986. The thirty-minute episode features one-on-one interviews with him and his wife Dora Kutesa in which they alternately recount his years of alcohol abuse, the failure of his liver and kidneys, and Dora's donating 75 percent of her liver to him after he spent four months in a coma in a hospital in New Delhi. Behind them are images of breezy gardens and a waterfall, and as they speak soft flute music plays in the background. During an interview in July 2015, an official in the Ugandan Ministry of Health, who had been chiefly responsible for working on the proposed National Alcohol Policy, cited Kutesa's experience and testimony as the chief cause of the president's increasing attention to alcohol in his speeches. With this in mind, Kutesa's story can be seen both as filling out the image of the redeemed potential of former alcoholics for a more generalized Ugandan public and as playing a special role in relation to President Museveni's interest in acting to create change around alcohol production because of their long-standing friendship.

The singularity of this particular instance of celebrity biography works alongside other more mundane testimonials offered by successful individuals in recovery from alcoholism and lifestyle and health columns instructing readers how to help alcoholic partners (Kemigisha 2009), explaining the links between alcohol and liver damage (Ssenkaaba 2009), and even works of serial fiction describing one man's experience at a rehabilitation center (Ortega 2012). Whether these articles are found in newspapers or in more focused publications, such as the magazine produced by a peer support organization, all are targeted at the expanding English-speaking middle class and aim to define elite drinkers as potential patients and their family members as potential conduits to treatment.

Articles like "From an Alcoholic to Academic Ace" (Okiror 2009) speak to specific concerns over elite forms of student drinking. While youth access to alcohol has always been an important issue in East Africa (Willis 2002), the current concern that these stories point to differs from those of the colonial and precolonial eras. This is not a question of adults holding onto a threatened monopoly on alcohol as a technique and symbol of power. Instead, we see parents desperately trying to prevent their children from squandering the investments they've made. By the time their children have reached university, parents have poured tremendous resources into their educations, and they expect to recoup these costs through their child's ability to help other members of the family, or at very least to be able to take pride in what their children have made of their lives. When alcohol abuse stands in the way of this achievement, it is not a matter of trying to stop a young person from jumping rank by accessing beer through purchase rather than through the gift of an elder; instead it is an attempt to avoid the tragedy of wasted potential.[4] While the cost of attending Lakeview easily matches university tuition, the expense may seem worth it to families looking to recuperate such a massive potential loss.

The specter of wasted potential is perhaps most poignantly realized in the figure of the student who has "drunk his fees." Over the course of our work on this project, Ugandan friends told us many versions of this story as they affirmed our interest in attending to the importance of addressing problem drinking in Uganda. Within a few days of her first trip, a young priest who was training to be an addiction counselor told China a story of a mother who had looked at the previous week's *New Vision* newspaper, expecting to find the name of her son among the list of students expected to graduate from Makerere University the following week. She looked and looked but could not find his name. The next morning, the mother went to the administrative offices at the campus to find out what had happened. "We stopped seeing your son in the second year," the secretary said. "The first year he came, the second year he came and had some retakes, but then we didn't even see him. You know, these students start using drugs so they can read and concentrate, but then. . . ." The women eventually confronted her son and learned that instead of paying his fees, he would go straight to the bar with the money and deposit it there to drink with it for the whole term.

It is not only these extreme instances of wasted resources that make families worry. Elite families may also come to recognize that there is a problem when their children have graduated and started working but are failing to contribute to the welfare of other family members. As one of the counselors at Lakeview explained, "Families have spent so much money and so much time investing in these kids and they are expecting them to contribute to the family income or to [be] helping others in the family or at least to [be] helping the family by making progress, showing that their investments in them have paid off. When this doesn't happen, it is a real sign that there is a problem."

The high levels of education and family wealth of those who attended rehabilitation centers during our research presented unique challenges for their recovery efforts. Many struggled with the difficulty of feeling like they hadn't reached where their friends from school had and fearing that they never would. The older clients at Lakeview, who had previously worked in major positions as bankers and lawyers, felt deeply ashamed about the loss of those jobs, their sense of identity still attached to an elite status that now seemed irrecoverable.

The elite backgrounds of the majority of the patients at both Butabika and Lakeview also shaped the culture of the AA groups and other peer support recovery organizations. English was the sole language used in Kampala's AA meetings, and other social gatherings and conversations often involved sophisticated humor and wordplay with references that would have been impossible to follow without an advanced degree. While we delighted in these jokes and the laughter that followed, these language games also made it clear who could and could not participate in this rarefied milieu. The world that people in recovery were building with one another through gathering, meeting, and in-jokes was a precious and jealously guarded space where people could both be honest about their struggles while also enjoying the company of other elites. That said, it could be a difficult space for people like Maurice, who sometimes felt that the ideal of successful recovery was painfully out of reach. If this space felt awkward for people like Maurice, who at least had a foot in the world of people who went to university, held high-paying jobs in the government or formal sector, spoke English with their friends, and spent their leisure time in malls, it was even more unlikely that someone who had never reached university, who worked in the informal sector, and who generally spoke with their friends, family, and coworkers in one of Uganda's many local languages would feel at ease in an AA meeting. This observation was one shared by many people in recovery. They wanted to reach out to people beyond their own circles to share the ideas and practices that had benefited them, and they struggled to think beyond the forms of literacy that were central to AAs "Big Book"—no matter what language it might be translated into. But finding ways to do this that would also protect the fragile shelter of a recovery community still in the making is something that was yet to be accomplished.

MAURICE

In March 2018, China arrived in Uganda again, and on her first day back we all went to try to find Maurice in the ghetto. Gingerly traversing the muddy back lanes, we arrived at the veranda of the shop only to find that Maurice was gone. The other men on the veranda told us that Maurice had gone off to some church. We realized that they were talking about the African Peace Center (APC), a newly opened day center located in a private house that was donated to the founder by his parents.

After winding through the unmarked roads for what seemed like hours in the suburban neighborhood where the center is located, we eventually arrived at a red metal gate at the end of a small side street. A large commercially printed banner read "African Peace Center–APC." The name gave no indication of the purpose of the center, which both ensured the privacy of those who visit and limited, intentionally or unintentionally, the reach of the center. None of the *boda boda* drivers we asked along the way for directions had any idea what we might be talking about. This was a protected space for people who were already part of a relatively closed community.

We rang the bell on the gate, and after it opened we drove through to find a solid stucco bungalow with a tiled roof and large windows surrounded by a neatly manicured lawn and several large palm trees. We were all tired after what had already been a long day moving around the city, and the cool breeze of this hilltop neighborhood immediately refreshed us.

Inside the glass French doors, there were four new sofas arranged in a rectangle around a large coffee table. There was art on the walls and a bookcase sparsely filled with a few books. A television was conspicuously absent. The intentionality of this absence was quickly pointed out by one of the counselors: "We could have easily afforded one, but the quiet is important." On the sofas, three men sat silently, reading AA books to themselves. One never spoke. The second, wearing high lace-up hiking boots, occasionally addressed us in American-accented English. The third was Maurice.

Maurice spoke to us softly but clearly, his hands shaking lightly as he talked. He looked small and thin in a dark plaid shirt and jeans, his woven belt pulled to the last notch. Despite being in withdrawal, his eyes sparkled, and he seemed happy to talk.

"We first went to the ghetto to find you," said George. "Your friends told us to look for you here."

"Yeah, the last time you saw me, Sarah gave me the number of a friend in AA. I called him and he brought me here. I've been coming every day but Sunday since."

"Do you come here on foot?" George asked.

"Whatever comes first. If I have the money, I board a taxi, but otherwise I walk. I try to stay here all day, so that I am not tempted to drink. I can be here during the day and then at night I go back there, keep to myself, and then in the morning I can come back here. At night in the ghetto, I try to hide in a different bar where people don't know me, where they will be less likely to try to buy me a drink, reading my AA book until it is late. Once it is late, I go back to that bar where you found me to sleep on the veranda. During the day, I can deal with the withdrawal symptoms all right, but at night, I dream. The dreams are the worst part. I dream of snakes wanting to bite me and I wake up. After five minutes I sleep again but see lions chasing me. Those are part of the withdrawal. When it rains, we just open an umbrella under the awning of the veranda to protect ourselves, but it doesn't help much. I will be okay. During the day, I don't get scared to sleep, because there is light. But at night, because we sleep outside, I sometimes think that the snake is for real. I do all right as long as I can come here during the day, but on Sunday, this place is closed, and I don't have anywhere I can go."

We thought for a while together about where else he could go at night. "Maybe there is a church that would allow you to sleep on the grounds," Sarah suggested.

"There are, but they are very far from here," Maurice replied.

Despairing, Maurice blamed himself for his drinking. "No one poured liquor down my throat," he said, flipping through his AA Big Book to find the story where this quote comes from. "There is no one else to blame for my drinking and the problems it has caused in my life. I need to work hard in recovery now to put my life back together."

As we got ready to leave, China wanted to find a way to give him 5,000 UGX for taxi fare and a meal, but Sarah worried that giving him that much money might also trigger a relapse. After much discussion we decided to give the money to the counselor, so that he could give it to Maurice slowly to facilitate his travel to and from Rubaga Cathedral, where he hoped he might find a place to sleep.

PARTNERS IN CRIME

The daily training sessions at Butabika constituted one of the most important aspects of the program, and we were encouraged to participate in these sessions as often as possible. The content of these sessions varied a bit, but typically focused on explaining the physical dangers of alcohol and cigarettes and helping patients learn strategies for avoiding temptation and negotiating sobriety. Many of these strategies focused on meeting the need to reorganize one's relationships and, crucially, to avoid spending time with the people with whom one used to drink.

As Sarah, then a volunteer trainer at Butabika, told a group of patients one Tuesday morning, "Your partners in crime will be aggressive, they will want to pull you back. Your partners will try to pull you back. They will always want you to be at their same level. They will be saying, 'How can she move away from us? We want her to be the same.' They will even try mixing it into some of your drinks. You must try to reconsider and find other ways of dealing with it." Over and over again, the patients were advised to change their friends, what they did with their time, their way of dressing, even their routes for reaching home so that they would not pass by their old drinking spots.

This way of talking and thinking about the need for a person in recovery to change their "people and places" might sound so familiar that you scarcely give it a thought. But the challenge of doing this when social connection is the foundation upon which everything else is built is rarely acknowledged by the people leading these discussions. As we saw in the last chapter, those "partners in crime" may have also been the people with whom one has lived and worked and who one has relied on for meeting most basic needs. In Uganda, being together, being part of one another (Eisenstein 2021), constitutes the necessary condition for experiencing a sense of well-being and for securing basic necessities. With regard to the latter point, the limits of Uganda's governmental and nongovernmental social safety nets result in a situation where there are no shelters, no halfway houses, no soup kitchens, no unemployment offices. Anyone who needs to find a place to stay, food to eat, and eventually a job, will have to depend on friends and family.

With friends redefined as "partners in crime," people in recovery often turn to family. While we saw families provide housing, food, and connections to jobs over and over again, these relations were also shadowed by feelings of mutual resentment and suspicion on both sides, and these feelings of mistrust could be amplified by a disease model that posited addiction as a more or less permanent condition.

These relations were further strained by the fact that some people were taken to the treatment programs at both Lakeview and Butabika by force. Prospective patients were sometimes tricked into coming, told that they were being taken to buy land, to go out to eat, or to go to the beach, and then were surprised when they arrived at the center. In one instance, a university student admitted to Lakeview was left holding his mother's handbag. She told him that she would be back for it in a minute, but she never returned, and when he opened the bag, he realized it was empty. Another man, a middle-aged business lawyer, was left at Lakeview and not told who was paying to keep him there. In other cases, the parents of prospective clients told them where they were going, but that they would only need to stay for a week or two, not the ninety days the Lakeview program would really require.

These moments of force were not, of course, the only points of tension between people in recovery and their families. Experiences of injury and betrayal usually preceded the drinking problem, and they followed after treatment too. People who had moved through the recovery programs at Butabika and Lakeview often found themselves living with family members who they felt were watching their every movement, constraining their actions, and waiting for them to fail.

At the end of one of the morning training sessions at Lakeview, George crossed the compound to go and visit with the clients who were drinking tea and washing their silverware at the outdoor sinks commonly called "the beach." Over the talk of the others, George spotted Peter sitting alone and taking a cup of tea with a banana. He was surprised to see him, having ridden along with Peter to Kampala just a few weeks before when he was being discharged. One of the other men who was admitted just after Peter joked that Peter used to be his senior, but now he is Peter's senior. George pulled up a chair and sat down to talk.

"What happened?" George asked. "You had gone to your sister's house, right?"

"Yeah, I drank. I had become annoyed. My sister was following me, nearly looking under my bed to see if there were tot packs there. They were all over the place, but they belonged to the caretakers of the house. She was trying to turn my after-rehab into a rehab, monitoring all of my movements. I am a responsible adult! I have children at university! Yet, my sister wanted to manage every minute of my day. She wanted me to jog during the evening and I wanted to jog in the morning. I don't like the afternoon heat; I like it in the morning when it is cool. Can you believe that she even wanted to audit the time I go out jogging?"

"She doesn't work?" George asked, wondering how this woman had so much time on her hands.

"She's retired. Even to go and greet my mother, she said 'It is not necessary.' These counselors at Lakeview poisoned her mind, telling her things about me that weren't true, directing her to be strict with me.

"Even at church, as they were collecting the offertory, she pulled out money and gave it to me. I said, 'No, I have my own money.' When she saw the money she asked, 'Where did you get that money?' How can she ask me that? I have a bank card from Stanbic Bank and Bank of Africa. I have a pension. How do you ask me where I got the money from? She treats me like I'm a street kid on Kampala Road asking for a coin. I thought about packing up my bags. I was so annoyed."

"So, you went to a bar?" George asked.

"No," he said. "I went to an old friend. An old family friend who has sons who drink."

While relatives paid for expensive stays at Lakeview and provided critical resources of food and housing following discharge, many, like Peter, felt that these resources came at the cost of constant surveillance and judgment. People like Peter chafed against the control and the infantilization that came with it: "I have a pension and a child in university. And you ask me where I got money from?"

Another possible solution to this problem of isolation and the need to establish new networks of trust and social support were the Alcoholics Anonymous fellowships themselves. Yet, while some people managed to find friends through these meetings, many others mentioned the limited nature of this community of support. People come to meetings but leave immediately after. Those with cars drive away, while those without are left to find their own way home, often walking long distances due to lack of money for transport. Support is focused on working the steps and avoiding relapse, with little opportunity for making more practical sorts of connections.

This is not accidental. AA makes a firm distinction between social support and material support. Members of AA fellowships can, and should, support one another emotionally, both within and outside of the meetings. People frequently called one another by phone, checked up on one another by text, spent time together socially outside of fellowship meetings, and occasionally went out of their way to go and visit someone in person when they were in an acute state of crisis. But more material forms of support are strictly prohibited, justified with appeals to AA's explicit valuation of self-sufficiency.

Readers familiar with Uganda and many other parts of sub-Saharan Africa will likely be struck immediately by the incongruences of this firm line between the social and the material and the forms of friendship that define everyday life. In Uganda, sharing with one's friends, neighbors, and relatives is a moral imperative. This does not mean that society is egalitarian—far from it—or that one needs to give to the point of impoverishing oneself, but to withhold resources from a friend in need is considered to be immoral, even cruel (Scherz 2014). While prohibitions on material support might allow people in different economic situations to come together without wealthier members needing to worry about the fiscal implications of the relationships that might emerge, the refusals, both explicit and implicit, can also feel cruel to those in acute need.

As you will remember, Maurice was left to walk from the ghetto to the APC on a daily basis on an empty stomach. Even when others were eating at APC, no one offered to share their food with him. And certainly, no offers of housing were made. There were many nights when the prohibitions on material support left him in both physical and emotional pain and left him materially reliant on precisely those same "partners in crime" that he had been instructed to avoid.

MAURICE

In April 2018, Sarah went out to find Maurice again. She hadn't seen him at the APC in a while and suspected that she might be able to find him at J's shop in the ghetto. It had been raining and the place was soaked, the trenches that line the paths filled to the top with dirty water. After sitting with the men at the shop for a few minutes, she felt a tap on her shoulder and turned around to find Maurice, dressed in a dirty red t-shirt and denim shorts, hiding behind a shop door. As he came to sit on the bench next to her, he started to cry, holding her tightly, smelling strongly of alcohol.

"Maurice, what happened?"

"Sarah, I walk up to APC every day on an empty stomach, keep there the whole day on an empty stomach, walk back here at night, do the same the next day, and over and over again. Truly, what do you expect? I got someone's phone and called my brother to at least buy me some *posho* (cornmeal), beans, groundnuts, and charcoal and put them at APC. There's a charcoal stove. I can cook for myself, get something to eat and then come back here at night. I don't need much. But my brother just kept quiet on me."

They walked together for a while, trying to reach his brother by phone, but he wasn't picking up the calls. Maurice asked Sarah for some money, but Sarah, having just seen Maurice try to bargain with a food seller to give him alcohol later instead of the full lunch Sarah was trying to buy for him, refused, saying that the little money she had with her was for her transport home. Before he left her, he promised to go back to the APC, and then disappeared into the rush of speeding cars.

ONCE AN ADDICT, ALWAYS AN ADDICT . . .

One of the defining features of the programming at the rehab centers and AA meetings in Uganda is the tension between efforts to teach people in recovery skills that will enable them to resist relapse and the sense that the temptation toward relapse will always exist for them because their addictions have permanently altered their biology. Given that the leadership at both centers was trained and mentored by US-based addiction specialists, it is unsurprising that the programming at both Butabika and Lakeview revolved around this understanding of addiction as a CRBD.

While carrying forward aspects of a research program that took off in the middle of the twentieth century, the CRBD model did not fully coalesce in America until the 1990s.[5] In his seminal 1997 paper "Addiction Is a Brain Disease, and It Matters" Alan Leshner, who was at that time the director of the National Institute on Drug Abuse in the United States, defined the CRBD model and argued for the urgency of its acceptance by policymakers and the general public, for whom the idea that addiction is "a chronic, relapsing disease of the brain is a totally new concept" (1997, 46). Leshner argued that two decades of neuroscientific and behavioral research had shown that "prolonged drug use causes pervasive changes in brain function that persist long after the individual stops taking the drug," making the addicted brain "distinctly different from the non-addicted brain" (46). As opposed to earlier models, which Leshner saw as stigmatizing drug users or focusing on the need to help people through the period of acute withdrawal, the CRBD model sought to reframe addiction as a chronic illness that could be managed, but rarely cured. Given the long-lasting effects of drug use on "brain metabolic activity, receptor availability, gene expression, and responsiveness to environmental cues," Leshner argued that successful drug treatment could result in "a significant decrease in drug use and long periods of abstinence, with only occasional relapses," but that a permanent cessation of compulsive drug-seeking was an unrealistic goal.

Since this time, the CRBD model has been the guiding force in most NIDA-funded addiction research in the United States and has been the model at the center of many landmark articles and special issues. While not as uncontested as NIDA claims (Courtwright 2010), NIDA's call for broad public acceptance of the CRBD model in the United States has spread beyond the pages of scientific journals, with talk of hijacked brains and fluorescent images of fMRI scans flashing across American television screens and informing the curricula on addiction in American classrooms (Campbell 2007, 2010). While we do not aim to contest the neuroscience that informs this approach, we do follow the lead of researchers who have explored the harms this model can inflict upon those who have been diagnosed (Garcia 2010; Hammer et al. 2013), harms that are now spreading beyond the United States as this model gains international acceptance.

Patients and their families at Lakeview and Butabika were consistently instructed that addiction was a chronic disease, likened to diabetes, cancer, and HIV. They were constantly reminded that "a recovered alcoholic is not a cured alcoholic." "There is no cure," they said. "You are always an alcoholic." At Family Saturdays at Lakeview, parents were told that alcohol had permanently changed their children's brains and that these changes could never be reversed. Clients in Lakeview classrooms were encouraged to "get used to the disease," to remain consistent in their efforts to avoid relapse and to be constantly vigilant. "An addict can never truly be relaxed," the counselors said. Closing a session for new patients at Butabika, Sr. Nantambi reminded them of the importance of the closing lines of the AA Serenity Prayer, "Help me to accept the things that I cannot change." "It is a journey; remember. Once an addict you remain an addict, even when you are sober," she said. At times, the mark that was being put upon their characters extended beyond their propensity to relapse. One patient remembered one of the therapists they had met during their time in a rehab center telling them that alcoholics were liars. "You addicts will do anything. You'll lie, cheat, steal, just for a drink." While people, and not only people recovering from addiction, do indeed lie, these words reverberate in the social space of the recovery community, where accusations of lying and despair can add to the difficulty of regaining trust, shaping many social interactions.

While Maurice's parents and the friends he had made through AA hoped that one more stay at rehab might be enough to set him right, at least for a while, the cycle of relapse and return that shaped Maurice's life is also part of the story of addiction as a chronic condition without end (Garcia 2010). In other therapeutic pathways, failure may be diagnostic, pragmatically indicating that the next step on the quest for therapy for this particular illness lies elsewhere (Whyte 1997; Janzen 1982). By contrast, the CRBD model is unfalsifiable. When someone relapses again and again, it is, at least in part, a verification of the diagnosis. Maurice and those around him hoped that he might be able to change, but this hope was tempered by the forms of vigilance fostered by the recovery programs themselves and a corresponding reluctance to fully embrace the possibility of change and to fully enter into materially substantial forms of friendship.

As with the question of class discussed above, this problem of social connection was one that some members of Kampala's recovery community acknowledged themselves. Greg, whose recovery was supported both by AA and by his active involvement in a Pentecostal church, wondered with us about the possibility of an African AA, one that would speak to the ethics of interdependence at odds with the strangely individualistic form of fellowship being proffered in the globalization of American twelve-step programs.

While reminders about the dangers of relapse can indeed prove to be crucial barriers against efforts to "test" the cure, or to return to "social drinking" after discharge, many of those who succeed in their vigilance also find themselves completely defined by their identity as addicts and alcoholics. While some found minimally compensated or voluntary work as counselors or AA group leaders in small rehabilitation centers or other spaces related to recovery, their lives revolved around efforts to find a way forward for themselves in ways that were almost completely defined by their past. Called by others in the recovery community to appear in radio, television, and newspaper stories about addiction, they were granted public recognition, but in a form that required the confirmation of their continued identification with addiction. This is not to say that these opportunities for work, community, and media attention were not appreciated; they were. But these opportunities also required an incessant reaffirmation of the person's status as an incurable addict, even as they celebrated the person's processual state of "being in recovery."

Readers in Europe, North America, and elsewhere have lived with the CRBD model as their primary framework for understanding drinking problems for many years now. Having come to accept this model, they may find it hard to suspend the naturalness of the idea of addiction as an incurable disease. Likewise, they might take for granted the need to maintain good "boundaries" not only with those in recovery, but really with anyone. With these assumptions in mind, the chapters that follow demonstrate that this is not the only framework that exists and argue that these other ways of thinking, which place an emphasis on the possibility of transformation and release, have the capacity to orient people toward time and social connection in very different ways.

3

Put Something in His Drink

Sensory Shifts in Kampala's Herbal Medicine Shops

MARKET

In mid-July 2018, Sarah and China were sitting with Nankya Elizabeth, tying short loops of raffia to the edges of baskets to prepare them for display in her small herbal medicine shop. China and Nankya had bought the baskets before dawn that morning at the herb market. With no traffic, they drove the distance between her shop and the market in less than five minutes. Even still, Nankya was anxious to get started and China struggled to keep up as Nankya picked her way expertly across the uneven ground and through the maze of stalls. China had been to this market before, around midday when it was nearly empty, its stall counters displaying little more than a thin layer of fine dust. But that morning, in the pale light of a crescent moon, it was bustling with vendors seated on the ground, their wares spread out before them on cloths. There were huge piles of herbs bundled together, stacks of small flat baskets, sticks of wood, sacks of wood chips, and piles of bark, along with heaps of fruit rarely seen in other markets in Kampala, everything fresh and shining.

Nankya moved quickly from vendor to vendor, paying in advance for things she would later return to collect. Using the light from her phone to illuminate the herbs and her folded wad of cash, she bought a tall stack of small flat baskets. She bought a bundle of the herb commonly given to adolescents for bathing to prevent body odor. She bought fresh green herbs that could be burned to call customers to a business that has refused to prosper. She bought long garlands of the flowering herb for preparing the herbal baths used by infants and adults alike to bring blessings to the bather. She bought a large pile of shaggy bark and chips of wood from the center of a tree that is used to treat syphilis. By the time the sun began to rise over the eastern hills of Kampala, China and Nankya were back at her shop. Soon after they returned, Sarah joined them and Nankya put China and Sarah to work cutting herbs and preparing the other items for display.

When business is good, the walls of her shop are lined with things for sale. There are short gray *mumbwa* sticks made of clay mixed with medicines. These sticks will be ground down and then mixed with water to be drunk by pregnant women as part of preparation for childbirth. There are hollow gourds for offering alcohol, honey, water, and fresh banana juice to the *balubaale*. There are pumice stones for smoothing dry skin. There are hollow sticks with holes through the length that can be used to smoke herb-laced tobacco in offering to the *balubaale* or to call customers to a business. Nankya's shop is located in an area known for sex work, so these pipes are often purchased by women seeking to use the smoke of the herbs to magically attract men to them. There are baskets of small objects, cowrie shells, coins, and bells used for divination. Underneath the glass counter, there are bundles of tobacco, dried herbs and small clear plastic bags of powdered herbs, and behind the counter, a cozy patch of vinyl, a plastic chair, and a small television.

Sarah and Nankya began to chop firewood on the cement veranda on the side of Nankya's building. Nankya's neighbor and tenant Emily asked Nankya to hold her new baby as she stirred a pot of *posho* for lunch. While neighbors often help one another with childcare, this baby was especially dear to Nankya, as she had treated Emily's husband, Mayanja, for problems with alcohol several years before he and Emily met. The experiences of Mayanja, and others who have used herbal aversion therapies as a means of addressing their problems with alcohol, lie at the center of this chapter.

MAYANJA

Mayanja grew up in a family of distillers in a village in the Central Region of Uganda. He started drinking waragi when he was fifteen and by Primary Six, he was drinking so heavily that he dropped out of school. His parents were worried about him and tried giving him herbal medicines to make him stop without his knowledge several times, but it never worked. He tended to fight a lot when he drank, and, after one particularly bad fight, Mayanja ran to Kampala to escape the police.

He had a brother in Kampala who was willing to house him, and he got a job roasting chicken in front of one of the biggest bars in Kampala's most popular nightlife district. The brother told him that he would care for him, clothe him, house him, and feed him on the condition that Mayanja would save the money he earned in a savings box. But after moving to the city, being surrounded by bars, and starting to earn some money, his drinking only progressed. He spent everything he earned and ran up huge debts at all of the local bars on top of that. There wasn't one where he didn't have a debt. After a year, his brother asked to see the savings box. Sheepishly, he opened it and his brother found only 20,000 UGX inside. His brother was furious and told Mayanja that he could not take care of him anymore.

Without anywhere to stay, Mayanja started sleeping outside on the streets. He also started driving a *boda boda* for someone else. Since he had so little money, he slept on the seat of the borrowed motorcycle. A friend of his advised him to get a loan to buy his own *boda boda* and somehow, he managed to secure the loan. He had 300 USD in hand and was ready to go to buy the bike in the morning when he passed his friends in a bar. They called to him and bought him a bottle of Nile beer, and then another. He too, ordered a round for them. It soon became night and with "the beer on his head," he bought round after round. He was there for two days straight, buying for his friends. At the end, he had spent all of the money. In despair and frantic to make back his money, he picked up a man and a woman who were looking for a ride. At a traffic light, he lost control of the bike, and the woman didn't survive the accident.

Soon after he recovered from his own injuries following the accident, the microfinance officers began looking for him to pay back the loan. He ran to the village to avoid them, and his fellow group members were forced to repay the loan on his behalf. After two years in the village, Mayanja came back and one of his friends gave him a job roasting chicken again. His friends from the microfinance group found him there and asked his employer to pay them 5,000 UGX every day before paying him as a slow way of repaying the loan they had paid off for him. Eventually, they took pity on him and forgave the loan in its entirety.

Mayanja was still drinking at this time. But in 2012, a friend of his who owned the bar where he often drank told him that she knew of someone who could help him stop drinking, and she brought him to Nankya's shop, which is located near her bar. Nankya asked Mayanja if he wanted to stop drinking, and he told her that he did. He paid her 50,000 UGX, and she gave him an herbal mixture and told him to put it in alcohol and drink it. He drank it and vomited for days, but once he recovered, he found that when he tried to drink, it smelled terrible and he could not swallow it. Though Mayanja continues to spend time with his friends in bars, he has not drunk alcohol since taking the herbs Nankya gave to him.

HERBAL MEDICINE

The people you met in chapter 2 who had attended programs at Butabika and Lakeview were encouraged to see themselves as new kinds of people: as alcoholics, as addicts. At the rehab centers and AA meetings they attended, they were encouraged to draw on the strength that they might find in a higher power and in a community of fellow alcoholics to resist a lifetime of future temptations, which they were told would never truly cease. By contrast, Mayanja and others who seek out care from herbalists like Nankya, whether for themselves or for those they love, are introduced to a different understanding of problem drinking and its alleviation.

While some variation exists between different herbalists, in Nankya's care Mayanja was given powerful herbal emetics intended to induce intense bouts of vomiting. This process was thought to be capable of permanently transforming his sensory relationship to alcohol, causing it to smell terrible to him. He was told that drinking again could cause the vomiting to return even more violently.

In Mayanja's case, he sought out this treatment himself; the act of purchasing and enduring this treatment, which is costly in multiple senses of the word, served as a kind of bodily promise to himself that laid down a new set of criteria for future action (Lambek 2015). The body itself would be the judge of whether he kept this promise. In other cases, this treatment is administered by those connected to the drinker—usually wives, mothers, and sisters—without the drinker's knowledge or consent. Given the intense pain and discomfort of the vomiting this treatment is intended to bring, such forms of covert administration bind violence and care, force, and love, more tightly together than many readers might find comfortable.[1]

Whether the treatment is taken willingly or not, this bodily form of therapy can create profound shifts in the ways drinkers experience and engage with alcohol. Yet despite this powerful interruption of sensual experience, this form of treatment does not require a transformation of identity or even a transformation of social relationships. As you will see more fully below, Mayanja still spent time with his old friends, both in bars and at home, and still bought beers and waragi for them as he sipped his soda. Exploring this therapeutic pathway not only allows us to revisit an international debate on aversion therapy (Raikhel 2016), it also allows us to explore the relationship between cure and chronicity, the thought that a transformation of drinking practices need not be tied to a shift in identity, and the possibilities for friendships in recovery that lie beyond the bonds and boundaries of states of shared affliction.

Before returning to Mayanja and the specificities of aversion therapy, we pause for a discussion of the landscape of herbal medicine in Uganda as it looked during the first decades of the twenty-first century. Herbal medicines are an important aspect of the ways that people care for their well-being and the well-being of others in Central Uganda. Preparations made of both plants and minerals are taken in many forms. They may be consumed orally as teas and juices extracted from various fruits and leaves. Fresh and dried plants might be added to water to create herbal baths. They might be mixed into salves to be applied topically. They might be combined with clay and then mixed with water to be drunk. Or they might be smoked in pipes or burned on the fire. Some of these preparations are oriented primarily toward the treatment of physical ailments that correspond to biomedical categories like malaria, high blood pressure, or syphilis. Other treatments target less physical aspects of well-being, such as the assurance of blessings and the removal of *bisirani*, chronic bad luck. Some, such as the *kyogero* baths commonly prepared for infants, combine elements of both. Simple treatments can be prepared at home by people who have the knowledge and access to herbs growing near their homes (Whyte 1997). While people preparing treatments at home might not be considered herbalists or traditional healers, they nonetheless constitute an important part of the therapeutic landscape. In addition to the herbs people might mix for themselves at home or acquire from their mothers, grandmothers, and neighbors in the villages, people also avail themselves of the opportunity to visit a diverse range of specialists who prepare and sell herbal medicine in more formal settings (Obbo 1996).

In Kampala, the diversity of these practitioners plays out along multiple axes: their relative interest in placing their practice under the sign (both figuratively and literally) of research, the size of their business, the professional networks they participate in, the means through which they have come to their knowledge of herbal medicine, their involvements with Christianity or Islam, and perhaps most controversially, the degree to which they align or distance themselves from spiritual and magical means of healing.

The distance that can be opened between herbal medicine and more spiritual or magical forms of healing can be seen most clearly in the work of scientists at the Natural Chemotherapeutic Research Institute (NCRI). NCRI is a government funded laboratory focused on strengthening traditional healing systems, on expanding awareness of the nutritional properties of traditional Ugandan foods, and on researching the safety and efficacy of plant-based medicines. They are also interested in standardizing these products for both domestic use and for the creation of new "value added" products for export. These efforts aim both to serve Uganda's needs for safe affordable medicines and allow for Uganda's enhanced participation in global markets, a dynamic that mirrors the situation in many African countries (Langwick 2015).

While similar projects have been underway for decades in countries like Ghana and Tanzania (Osseo-Asare 2014; Langwick 2010), efforts to test and standardize herbal medicines in Uganda did not begin in earnest until the late 1980s when President Yoweri Museveni's National Resistance Movement (NRM) government began looking for ways to control the field of traditional medicine (Peterson 2016). At this time, the practice of traditional medicine was rapidly expanding to meet the twin challenges posed by a collapsing health system and the mounting AIDS epidemic. Expansions and innovations in this field of practice were part of an effort to meet the demands of the present moment through the preservation of *ebyaffe*, "our things," our heritage (Obbo 1996).

Yet, as part of their larger anti-superstition ideology, the members of the NRM government argued that the metaphysical aspects of traditional medicine were distracting people from the serious problems facing the country (Peterson 2016). In an effort to manage the situation, they looked to Tanzania and took inspiration from their efforts to standardize and commercialize herbal medicines to benefit the national health care sector and the national economy (Langwick 2015). The association of traditional healers known as Uganda N'eddagala Lyayo (Uganda and its medicines) had been active since 1962 (Illiffe 1998; Hoesing 2021); in 1988 the Ministry of Health declared that it would be the *only* association of traditional healers that would be recognized by the government. Uganda N'eddagala Lyayo's leadership worked actively with government officials to "[take] herbs and other botanical objects out of their occultist and metaphysical contexts and [place] them in the pharmacy," Derek Peterson writes, thus "[constituting] traditional medicine as a creditable analogue to western biomedicine" (2016, 797). In so doing, the NRM government and their allies at Uganda N'eddagala Lyayo were creating a new version of traditional medicine and making powerful claims about which entities had a right to exist in Uganda (Langwick 2010; Mol 2003; Droney 2017).

The current director of research for the NCRI, Dr. Caroline Akello, is continuing this process by actively seeking to define herbal medicines as objects that can be isolated from spiritual elements. When we met with her at the NCRI offices in May 2018, she noted her interest in testing "extracts," gesturing toward the brown liquids that filled the small white plastic jerry cans by the door, while expressing a hope for a holistic approach. In their efforts to extract herbs from their context, to scrape them clean of magic and metaphysics, Dr. Akello, the NRM government, and the NRM government's collaborators at Uganda N'eddagala Lyayo are seeking to define herbal medicine as separable, extractable, from its possible spiritual associations, and further, to claim that other, more mystical forms, have no right to exist.[2]

That said, while the leaders of Uganda N'eddagala Lyayo may have been happy to cooperate with the NRM government in the late 1980s and early 1990s, relations between healers, healers' associations, and the government remain quite complex. Over the course of our research, the practice of herbal medicine was in the process of coming under increased regulation through an attempt to pass the Traditional and Complementary Medicines Bill (2019). According to the Ministry of Health, this bill was designed to stop "quacks who masquerade as herbalists" from selling "concoctions that have been found to have no capacity to cure" (Segawa 2019). If implemented, a council would be responsible for giving licenses to herbalists, and to obtain these licenses, herbalists would need to submit their medicines to the NRCI to have their treatments tested for safety and efficacy and then to the National Drug Authority (NDA) for final approval. This approach to herbal medicine corresponds with the shift toward an evidenced-based practice of traditional medicine in Africa, presently advocated by the World Health Organization (World Health Organization 2013). Despite shared concerns with safety, the requirement that herbalists freely share information about the contents of their medicines was a source of great concern. The head of the National Council of Traditional Herbalists Association (NACOTHA) argued that the bill failed to provide any safeguards that would protect the knowledge and innovation of the herbalists and that this could result in the theft of their knowledge by local and foreign researchers. While the bill does state that a committee on intellectual property rights will be formed, many herbalists remain skeptical.[3]

As with the government's earlier work with Uganda N'eddagala Lyayo, this bill also excludes the practices of herbalists who have maintained an interest in more metaphysical means of healing. These exclusions were mirrored in Dr. Akello's own practices through which she endeavored to reconcile her interests in herbal medicine with her training as a scientist and with her Catholic faith. In line with this, Dr. Akello spoke openly with us about her long friendship with Fr. Anatoli Wasswa, the Catholic herbalist and author of a locally published guide to the tricks purportedly used by traditional healers to fool their clients (Wasswa and Miirima 2006). While retaining an interest in products that remained relatively close to the whole plants' parts from which they were derived,[4] like Fr. Anatoli, Dr. Akello was emphatic about the need to extract what she saw as the good elements of herbal medicine from what she took to be their harmful and misleading spiritual ties.

If Dr. Akello and Fr. Anatoli can be seen to represent one end of the spectrum of contemporary herbal medicine with regard to the separation of material and spiritual elements, Nankya represents the other. Despite her possession of a worn membership certificate issued by Uganda N'eddagala Lyayo, her practice combines the use of herbs for the cure and prevention of physical ailments as well as the use of herbs for spiritual protection, blessings, and other magical ends. Her means for discerning what herbs might be effective combine a pragmatic approach of trial and error with an epistemology of dreaming and inherited knowledge. Nankya also works closely with her sister, who is frequently possessed by several different spirits. During the course of our work with her, the two sisters invested a substantial sum of money in a ritual designed to move the *jjembe* spirit Lubowa from the head of the sister into the horn of a water buffalo (see Beattie 1969). Once moved, Lubowa could be made to perform tasks across great distances, such as moving a resume for a job candidate to the top of a pile stacked on a manager's desk. The movement of Lubowa into the horn was indeed a major business investment for the sisters, as customers could be asked to pay substantial sums for such services. Nankya's network also extended to a business partner in South Africa to whom she sent various herbal preparations by post. In this case, her medicines also served as some of the desirable "culturally distant" products that are so actively sought after in many vernacular therapeutic contexts across sub-Saharan Africa (Rekdal 1999; Thornton 2017; Luedke and West 2006).

Despite these more complex and distant ventures, the majority of Nankya's clients came from the area immediately surrounding her shop. In addition to her work as a healer, she was a trusted confidante to many of those who visited her shop. Many of these customers were involved in sex work and most came for problems related to sexual and reproductive health. They also sought out her services to acquire more mystical substances that could augment their blessings and cast off curses that may have been placed upon them. Because of her abilities to combine the material and the metaphysical, Nankya's patrons half-jokingly referred to her practice using the verb *okuloga*. While Ugandans commonly translate the word *okuloga* with recourse to the English verb "to bewitch," it lies closer to what anthropologists typically refer to as "sorcery" (Beattie 1963). Sorcery here refers to forms of magic that can be performed by anyone, provided that they have the technical know-how and the material items necessary. "Witchcraft," by contrast, is used by anthropologists to refer to an innate power that may harm others, even without the witch's conscious control. Witchcraft, in this sense, is relatively rare,[5] if not entirely absent, in Buganda. Sorcery, by contrast, is quite common and a subject of great debate and concern. All of this said, like Dr. Akello, Nankya also had to reconcile her practice as an herbalist with her practice as a Catholic, and did so in a way that allowed her rosary to sit in her shop drawer alongside the shells and coins sold to basamize for divination.

SOMETHING IN YOUR DRINK

Herbalists like Nankya and basamize, about whom you'll learn more in chapter 5, distinguish between two different kinds of drinking problems that roughly correspond to what Susan Reynolds Whyte has referred to as symptomatic and explanatory idioms (1997). The first of these, the symptomatic idiom, describes a way of treating illnesses and other misfortunes that attempts to bring "the power of substances (in terms of pharmaceuticals or African medicines) to bear on problems" (23) without seeking to identify a deeper, more relational cause. Being more straightforward and often cheaper, symptomatic treatments are typically the first resort. By contrast, the second, explanatory idiom seeks to identify and influence "a personalistic agent as a cause of affliction . . . [including] human cursers, sorcerers, shades of the dead, and spirits" (23). This second idiom seeks to identify "socially relevant" (Evans-Pritchard 1937) or relational (Thornton 2017) causes of misfortune. Addressing problems that have been defined through the explanatory idiom is often significantly more involved and not a process to be undertaken lightly.

While some of Nankya's treatments combine herbal and spiritual approaches to misfortune, the aversion therapies administered by healers like Nankya are not thought to be capable of curing drinking problems caused by personalistic agents, but are instead intended to work on the sorts of problems that arise when drinking that began as a response to stress, pressure, and poverty gets out of control. Drinking problems caused by "deeper" issues involving the *balubaale* are seen as requiring the intervention of basamize. While some herbalists, like Dr. Akello, eschew engagements with the balubaale entirely, this distinction, and the concomitant understanding that both kinds of problems exist, is held by both herbalists and basamize, and they divide their work accordingly. In the movement between these idioms, herbal medicines can also serve a diagnostic purpose, with their failure indicating that there are deeper problems that need to be addressed, although there were some who arrived at shrines to address the deeper problems without having first engaged in herbal treatments.

As noted above, the symptomatic treatment employed by Nankya, and sought out by people like Mayanja, relies on the use of an aversion therapy intended to permanently transform the patient's sensory experience of alcohol. In this therapy, a substance derived through the squeezing or pounding of parts of one or more plants is placed in a liquid for the patient to drink. Most commonly, this liquid is the patient's favorite alcohol. The herbs in the alcohol are intended to induce a period of vomiting that can last for several days. Sometimes the vomiting goes on for so long that the herbalist suggests that the patient be given sugar cane to stop the vomiting. The patient is told that if they try to drink again, they will not be able to stand the smell of alcohol and the vomiting will return, and indeed, people like Mayanja who were successfully treated said that after taking the medicine, alcohol smelled so terrible that it left them nauseated.

The use of emetics as a modality of healing might lead us to think that this form of care is focused on the balancing of different sorts of fluids within the body, as in humoral medicine, or focused on the expulsion of other sorts of toxins or spiritual potencies from the body. While these are often uses to which emetics are put, neither of these accurately describes the reasoning behind this form of treatment. Alternately, given the movement of fluid that follows the ingestion of an emetic, we might consider the rich literature in medical anthropology on the symbolism of bodily fluids and their movement (Taylor 1992; Turner 1967; Myhre 2019; Geissler and Prince 2010; Janzen 1992). That said, if symbolism is at all important in this case, it has more to do with the symbolism of the plant itself. The plant that is used in some preparations is also used in other contexts: to mark the boundaries of property; to symbolize the work of "cutting cases" in traditional courts; and to sprinkle the waters from herbal baths used to wash away bad omens before entering sacred spaces. It is, in all of these uses, a plant that powerfully symbolizes cutting, removal, and separation.

More important than the symbolic meaning of the plant, however, was the profound transformation of Mayanja's sensory experience of alcohol. Following his treatment by Nankya, Mayanja came to experience as disgusting the alcohol that he had previously desired. This, importantly, was not tied to a moral evaluation of alcohol. He didn't mind if others drank it and continued buying drinks for his friends. Rather, it became something that was physically nauseating to him personally. Changing his mind or coming to the realization that alcohol was something he should avoid was only the first step that brought him to Nankya's door. The more important shift occurred during the treatment itself, during which the vomiting reoriented his sensorium at a more bodily level.

The sensory nature of this technique demands that we shift our focus from the interpretation of symbols to the body's sensuous experience of the world

(Howes 2019). While the layered symbolic meanings of the plants used in some forms of treatment are indeed beautiful, Nankya never mentioned them and responded blandly to China's questions about the symbolic similarities between the different uses of the plant. She focused instead on the way the plants could allow for the recultivation of her patients' sensory engagement with the world.

This form of aversion therapy, in which a person is simultaneously given alcohol and a substance that results in vomiting, is neither unique to Uganda nor recent. The earliest written records for this technique date, indeed, to 77 CE (Smith 1982). If we may be permitted a brief digression, we might look to the well-known work on aversion therapy in Russia. In 1933, Russian researchers began exploring what they called "conditional reflex therapy" or "apomorphine treatment." Following closely on the work of Ivan Pavlov, these researchers sought to use the emetic apomorphine to condition an unconscious reflex that would make the patient nauseous when they tasted or smelled alcohol. Given the repressive political climate of the Soviet era, there were few critiques made at the time, but after apomorphine treatment fell out of favor in the 1980s and 1990s, physicians and researchers became more openly critical of the approach (Raikhel 2016, 14–19).[6]

While aversion therapies never became as common in the United States, they were explored in a series of clinical studies, most taking place between the 1940s and 1980s, with some reporting impressive results (McLellan and Childress 1985). These studies were carried out during an important moment of transition in addiction research in the United States. Despite their somewhat more systematic methods in their hopes of a cure, the scientists researching aversion therapies represented an earlier phase of addiction research. As we discussed in chapter 2, as the twentieth century progressed the CRBD model became more popular. With the rise of a paradigm holding that addiction was chronic and incurable, earlier modes of research that focused on developing cures for addiction became practically unthinkable.

Besides the impact of the CRBD model, other elements may have impacted the viability of this line of research after the 1990s. Movements advocating for the rights of patients, particularly in the field of mental health, likely played a role in the declining popularity of a treatment that was fundamentally based on inducing suffering. Popular films like Stanley Kubrick's 1971 *A Clockwork Orange*, which graphically depicted a fictional aversion therapy intended to curb violent behavior, may have also played a role in the increasing unthinkability of treatments based on reflex conditioning.

Like the American and Russian critics who opposed the acts of cruelty that seemed to lie at the center of aversion therapy (Raikhel 2016), some herbalists in Uganda have tried to develop new methods for treating addiction that do not rely on aversion. While some claimed to us that they have had success with these approaches, we were never able to meet their patients. While we do not deny the possibility of other herbal cures existing, the vomiting itself seems to be such an important part of the treatment undertaken by patients like Mayanja that we would have to classify herbal treatments not based on the induction of an aversion reflex as something else entirely.

In addition to the aversion reflex itself, there may also be a second element at play in cases like Mayanja's, namely that he knowingly sought out the treatment. While we heard many stories of people who had covertly been given alcohol mixed with herbs intended to make them vomit, we were never able to interview anyone who had been treated without consent. Aside from the objections an American-trained bioethicist might raise about administering an aversion therapy without a patient's consent,[7] there may also be elements of the treatment that result from the patient's own decision to undergo such a painful form of therapy. Might there be a sort of vow that is taken when someone commits their body to sobriety through the ingestion of a substance that they believe will make it impossible for them to drink in the future? In this, there is perhaps a kind of promise, a performative act that establishes the criteria against which all future action will be judged (Lambek 2010). If this is a promise, it is not a public one, as people rarely share their stories of this form of herbal medicine treatment beyond the circle of a few intimate others. Instead, it is a promise that is largely made to oneself. Further, given how the promise is made, it is one's own body, and its subsequent propensity to become nauseated by the smell of alcohol, that is held to be the future judge of the (former) drinkers' fidelity to their oath.

MAYANJA

On a rainy evening in November, George went to meet Mayanja near his home. When George reached the spot where Mayanja usually waited for customers with his fellow *boda boda* drivers, he was nowhere to be found. George called him on his phone. "There's too much rain for me to be out there waiting for customers," he said. "I'm up at Maureen's bar playing Ludo. Just ask anyone along the way and they can direct you to the place."

Maureen's bar was packed with men holding beer bottles and plastic cups of waragi and gathered around Ludo boards, some playing, others cheering them on. Mayanja was at the back of the room playing and drinking a glass bottle of Pepsi with a straw. Mayanja started to stand, and George told him that he didn't mean for his visit to interrupt the game. But Mayanja insisted that they should go somewhere quieter to talk, and the two left the bar to sit inside a nearby shop, both drinking sodas despite the cold wet weather.

As they sat, Mayanja started to fill George in on his various business ventures. He had just returned to town after having spent a week in his home village taking care of his tomato plants. He had planted a large number, timing it so that he would be ready to harvest and sell the tomatoes for a handsome profit during the Christmas season. This wasn't all. He went on to tell George that he had also started rearing hybrid "kroiler" chickens at the home of a friend. "I've already got 250 birds," he said proudly. Mayanja had met this friend while driving him on his *boda boda*. After Mayanja had driven him on a regular basis for some time, the man started to give him some small work with his screen-printing business. Impressed by Mayanja's dedication, he offered some space behind the small square bungalow that housed the screen-printing factory for the chicken-raising venture. By the next time we saw Mayanja in March 2018, he had sold the tomatoes and invested the profits in the chicken business, his urban flock growing to 600. His wife Emily was also preparing to give birth in a few weeks' time. By May, his wife was holding their tiny son when we went to visit them in their small one-roomed home behind Nankya's shop.

Even with all of his new business ventures, Mayanja has continued to drive his *boda boda*, but he has gone from being a man hopelessly in debt to being the owner of three *boda bodas* and the treasurer of his driving association (Doherty 2017). Most of his friends are still *boda boda* drivers, and nearly all of them drink. When he isn't working, Mayanja spends time with them in bars, and before he met his wife, he also bought beers for them to drink at his house while they watched movies on his television. These connections have been vital to his sense of well-being and his success in his various business ventures. Where the clients of Kampala's formal rehabilitation centers are told to avoid visiting bars and spending time with their former "partners in crime," Mayanja has continued his friendships with his former drinking companions. Mayanja's fear of the physical consequences that might follow if he chooses to drink again after taking the medicine likely make bars safer for him than they would be otherwise.

Further, while Mayanja now lives a very different kind of life, the transformation in his drinking has not been accompanied by a shift in his identity, in his understanding of himself as being or having been a particular "kind" of person (Hacking 1986). He understands that he can never drink again, but he does not see himself as an "alcoholic" or an "addict." Further, as opposed to the discussion of past regrets that often takes center stage in AA meetings or the idea that one's future might lie in the possibility of founding a rehabilitation center or getting a job in one, Mayanja is focused on his plans for his future in a way unrelated to alcohol—his work, his wife, his child. His primary focus is not on the inner self but is rather oriented outwards toward his current relationships and the things he is doing.

The staff at Uganda's rehabilitation centers do advise people in recovery to take up full and productive schedules to fill the endless expanses of time that will confront them on their return home. They instruct them in skills like liquid soap-making, charcoal briquette production, and catering that they hope might help them launch small businesses upon being discharged from the centers. Yet this advice also hinges on a suggestion that one ought to begin a completely new life, a life that doesn't involve time spent in bars and with the people one used to drink with. By contrast, Mayanja retained close ties with his friends and even kept up with his role of buying occasional rounds of drinks in bars and at home. At the same time, with very little of his own money, time, and mental energy being spent on alcohol, he was able to work hard and invest his earnings into a diverse portfolio of small businesses and into a life that includes a wife and child. Whatever status he may have lost as his own drink order shifted from beer to Pepsi, he regained by way of his growing financial security. Impressed with the progress he was making in his own life, and aware of the difficulty that his drinking had caused for them in the past, his friends didn't hassle him about the reasons he no longer drinks. Instead, they made him the treasurer of their association.

While we don't know what would have become of Mayanja if he had entered a formal rehabilitation program, we suspect that he might not have felt as secure about maintaining the relationships that served as the space within which he would eventually come to distinguish himself. We might also ask how these relationships would have changed if he had come to see himself as a particular kind of person, rather than simply as someone who no longer drinks.

The simplicity of the approach taken by herbalists provides a marked point of contrast with all three of the other approaches discussed in this book, all of which seek to attend to issues that are happening at a deeper level—whether that be the level of a brain that is irreversibly altered or the level of a soul that has come under the influence of spirits. In the following two chapters, we attend to how cases play out when deeper spiritual issues are thought to be involved: first, at the fellowship of Pastor John, and then at the shrine of Jjajja Kasumba.

4

Not You

Hoping for Deliverance
in Kampala's Pentecostal Churches

DANIELLA

Pastor John's church lies in a rapidly developing suburban area just south of Kampala. Outside the church, people crowd the street selling steamed cobs of maize and other snacks by the roadside. There are lines of white *matatu* taxis ready to ferry passengers to and from the central taxi parks of Kampala. In fact, there are so many taxis that this church could nearly be a taxi park in its own right. Across the road from the church is an open field; it is packed with cars, most of them large and in good repair.

On our first visit to the fellowship in 2018, all of this was new to George and China, but none of it was new to Sarah. She had been coming to this fellowship since she was a child. In those days, the place was still small. Pastor John established the fellowship as a Friday night home cell meeting in 1992. Just prior to this, in 1990, Pastor John had been living in London as a migrant worker. He says that while he was there he received a calling from God to return to Uganda to start a fellowship ministry that would be focused on deliverance and on building an army for God that could fight battles during the end times. Over the next ten years, the fellowship outgrew the garage where it met, and several other spaces after that. Eventually, the fellowship grew so large that its members decided to construct the building where it presently meets.

Upon reaching the church, we had to pass through a security checkpoint where a row of men and women were ready to check the contents of our bags (see Maxwell 2005). Behind the security checkpoint there was a large brick church, and through its open doors we could see rows and rows of white plastic chairs filling its floor and the balcony above. In front of the church, and all around it, were tents filled with more chairs to hold the people who come here each day to hear Pastor John's teachings.

On this day, we did not enter the church, but instead turned to the right, toward the administrative building. We entered the building and went up a narrow staircase to an office with two desks and a glass radio booth. Down the hall were other offices for the pastors, which have wood and glass windows instead of interior walls.

We waited for a while in the reception area. The chairs were scarce as there were many other people also waiting to see the pastors. Eventually, a young woman named Daniella came out to meet us. She was impeccably attired in a dress with a full skirt that stopped just past her knee, along with a red sweater and red high heels matching the red accents on her dress. Sarah introduced Daniella to George and China, and Daniella quickly took us all back down the narrow stairs to the hall below, her high heels clicking as she went.

We sat in the corner of the hall to talk, and there was a strong cool breeze coming in through an open window. Near the door, there was a large pile of luggage, maybe eight feet high and ten feet wide—suitcases, jerry cans, and sacks. Over the course of the conversation, China slowly realized that the luggage belonged to the people Daniella spoke about, people who sleep Monday through Friday at the church, leaving only on the weekend to go somewhere else.

Daniella told us that she herself had spent over two years sleeping at Pastor John's after having been referred to the church by a friend. When she first arrived, she had come to pray for a visa so that she could start her life over again in another country. At that time, Daniella was drinking very heavily. She had started drinking during her last year of secondary school. She started slowly, but by the time she reached university there was little she felt she could do without first taking a drink of the potent distilled spirit waragi. She would take it to class, serve it to friends, study while drinking, discuss while drinking. She was drinking in taxis, at home, cooking, washing. She was rarely without a bottle. Over time, alcohol started to create problems for her, and she found that she could not avoid drinking even when she knew she should. She missed job interviews or arrived drunk. Old friends were embarrassed to be seen with her. Her fiancé tried to help her to stop, but he eventually left her too.

When Daniella arrived at Pastor John's in 2014, she found that the teachings were very different from what she had expected, and she loved the way the pastors taught about forgiveness, anger, desperation, and frustration. Over time, Daniella came to think that even if she did go abroad, she would gain nothing, and so she decided to wait for God to change her, thinking that only then she would get somewhere in her life. She was still drinking at this time, but no one ever sent her away from church. She would come to church drunk to listen to the sermons and then leave to go back to her drinking. But over time she settled in and began listening to the teachings with more seriousness.

Eventually, in 2015, she decided to follow Pastor John's advice "to approach the altar of grace and mercy with boldness," to tell God that she was tired of drinking. In prayer she said, "You know what, God, I didn't want to become born again, but I came here. God, my life is a mess because of A, B, C, D. I've lost everything because of alcohol. I have discovered that I can't leave it on my own. You say, 'Come to me, you who were weary, and I shall carry the burden for you.' I don't want money. I don't want a husband. I want you to change me, to give me a new heart and to put your spirit in me.'"

She stayed in church and cried to God for ten days, praying and fasting. On the tenth day of this fast, Pastor John was at the pulpit. It was around two in the morning. Daniella had been crying and praying to God to change her when Pastor John began to speak, addressing no one in particular. He said, "You girl, you are here, and you always feel something is asking you for alcohol and you cannot contain it. You cannot contain it because it is *not you*. It is a spirit. Come up to the pulpit here. I will pray for you, for today is your day."

Even that day, Daniella had been drinking alone at home before coming to church, but nevertheless she went up to the altar and Pastor John prayed for her. The church was full to capacity, but she said she was not afraid of anyone. Daniella said that as Pastor John prayed, she felt something heavy moving from her toes upward until it went out of her. She said that on this same day, God also visited her in a dream. In the dream, God came in the form of Pastor John. She was very dirty and tired, and Pastor John looked at her. He did not touch her, but he looked at her, and the more he looked at her the more she became clean. Her clothes began to change too, and she saw herself transforming into a different person. When she woke up, she felt very happy and had no desire to drink.

"NOT YOU"

When Ugandan Pentecostals like Daniella and Pastor John speak of the pain and suffering of addiction as being caused by a spirit, they are not speaking metaphorically. For many of these Ugandan Christians, addictions are not *like* spirit possession, or slavery for that matter, in the sense that one has metaphorically lost control of one's agency to another. To be addicted *is literally* to be under the control of a being that comes from outside the self. As will be true in the stories of those who visit the shrines of the spiritual healers in the next chapter, many Christian practitioners of spiritual warfare see problem drinking as caused by spiritual forces,[1] or what some have called intangible persons (Thornton 2017). For these Christians, moving beyond problems with alcohol requires them to exorcise the spirit that is causing the problem through deliverance. As we will see in the next chapter, for participants in the mediumship rites carried out in shrines dedicated to the balubaale spirits, the task is not deliverance, but rather finding ways to better accommodate the spirits by recognizing them and moving into a more productive relationship of reciprocity with them.

At both the church and the shrine, this way of understanding problem drink-ing as something that results from the actions of spiritual others—others that are fundamentally non-self and separable from the self—also gives people a way of understanding and addressing problem drinking that offers them real hope, and this hope for the future offers different possibilities for engaging in the tasks of the present. As we noted in the introduction, Angela Garcia (2010) has power-fully described the devastating stakes of disease models that seem only to replicate the melancholic chronicity of endless loss in places where life has been shaped by acts of dispossession for generations. This chapter responds to Garcia's analysis of melancholic chronicity by exploring the lives of people who have understood their problems with alcohol in a radically different way. We seek to understand what these alternative framings of addiction—and the spiritual experiences and the new orientations toward life that accompany them—mean for people who have faced problems related to alcohol and how these understandings shape their relation-ships with others, both inside and outside of the church.

In so doing, this chapter builds directly on Helena Hansen's ethnography of Pen-tecostal addiction ministries in Puerto Rico (2018). Drawing on Cheryl Mattingly's writings on hope as a practice of actively trying to create a life worth living (2010), Hansen writes of these ministries as social technologies that see themselves as capable of effecting profound forms of transformation.[2] Building on this work, we argue that Pastor John's church allowed for new forms of hope that gave people like Daniella the capacity to act and endure.[3] The model of atonement that underlies the practices of spiritual warfare (Robbins 2020; Aulén 2010) also led the people of Pastor John's church to see Daniella, and others like her, as fundamentally separable from the spiritual forces that had caused her to drink. This gave Daniella, and those around her, hope for the future and opened a space for building trusting interper-sonal relationships. In short, the fact that her problematic drinking was seen as having been caused by agents who were both non-self and separable from the self afforded Daniella an opportunity to begin again (Scherz, Mpanga, and Namirembe 2022; Kirmayer 2004). The language of spiritual warfare and the practices of some Pentecostal addiction ministries can involve acts of violence or force that stretch our definitions of care to their limits (O'Neill 2019; Goldstone 2017). Yet the forms of spiritual experience and models of atonement fostered at Pastor John's were focused not on punishment and captivity, but instead on fostering hope and creat-ing spaces for practicing that hope through the formation of new social ties.

ETHICS BEYOND THE INDIVIDUAL

The fellowship's chief administrator, Pastor M., often took it upon himself to make time to chat with us when we came to visit the church. On an afternoon in July, Sarah and China went to visit him in his office on the second floor of the adminis-trative building. He was behind his desk working between two computer screens, preparing to give a lecture for his other job at a university where he teaches mathematics. On a large sheet of paper taped to the wall was a diagram showing many boxes of text lettered with a fine red pen. The boxes were joined together by lines with arrows showing the flow from one box to the next. The writing was so precise that it could have been an illustration for the mathematics lecture he was about to give at the university.

Sarah asked what the drawing was, and Pastor M. eagerly began to explain. "I was teaching when a certain military group came in here. They could relate to what I was teaching, for I was teaching about war. I was teaching them about the war in heaven and how it comes here. How the devils found themselves in this world. That's the structure of the war," he said, pointing to the diagram on the wall. He said that there had been a war in heaven, and in this war the devil was cast out into the world. Jesus then came to the world to fight the devil. In this way, the spiritual battle they had been fighting was extended from heaven down to earth. He explained, "America, Europe, Asia, Africa all have their demons. We can't tell the number we have on earth. The Bible tells us a third of the angels in heaven were cast out down here to earth, but we don't know the magnitude. Jesus was sent to fight them. That is why salvation is a spiritual warfare. Evil spirits actually affect all of us. Jesus refers to them as unclean spirits and by unclean he means that these spirits can do anything that's dirty, from promiscuity, murder, stealing, drinking and all sorts of sins that defile man. Poverty, sicknesses, and addiction all are caused by unclean spirits, but when you defeat that spirit, you become free."

He went on to explain that the world is just a mirror of what is happening in the spiritual realm and that spirits must be defeated in the spiritual realm before they can be defeated in our earthly realm. Since our world is just a reflection, we cannot change it by trying to fix it directly. It would be as if a man stood in front of the mirror trying to button his shirt by trying to manipulate the buttons that appeared in his reflection. "All of the problems here, you have to first fight them in the spirit. That's why you have to intercede through prayer. If you have a meaningful prayer of intercession, then you can change the whole world."

The metaphor of the mirror and Pastor M's diagram both point to a view of personhood, agency, atonement, and moral culpability that sees everything—from problems of world historical significance to issues like problem drinking—as being caused by the workings of demons. While a person's actions might unintentionally create openings for such non-human others to act in that person's life, or in the lives of other people related to that person, these non-human others can cause people to act in ways that quickly exceed their control and culpability. These demons are fundamentally "not me" and practitioners of this form of prayer believe that they can be defeated through ongoing intercession.

In both the churches and in the shrines, this way of thinking about problem drinking involves an understanding of the person as a relational (Comaroff and Comaroff 2001; Klaits 2010; Zigon 2021), passionable (Lienhardt 1961), permeable (Werbner 2011), exposed (Thornton 2017), dividual (Strathern 1988, Mosko

2010) being. Despite their subtle differences, these various heuristics overlap and intermingle and have all been used to describe a vision of the person that highlights the role other people, substances, and spiritual forces play in their constitution. While these concepts were developed in explicit contrast to individualism, it is perhaps more useful to think about this suite of concepts as existing in a more complex relationship with individualism, as terms in complex processes of negotiation, as modes of being that can entwine and alternate with one another depending on the situation (Bialecki and Daswani 2015; Daswani 2015, 2011; Pype 2011; Coleman 2011).

In this way, spiritual warfare discourse points to a radically different view of agency and moral responsibility from that contained in other Christian discourses of sin. For example, in the model of sin that theologians call the penal substitution model, humans are cast as fundamentally sinful beings whose sins would be rightfully punished by God, but for the death of Jesus (Robbins and Williams Green 2017; Robbins 2020). By contrast, what has been called the *Christus victor* model of atonement, commonly found in spiritual warfare discourse, attributes sinful actions to the workings of demons that come from outside the self, and that can be defeated through ongoing prayer and intercession (Gibson 2017; Gifford 2004; Aulén 2010; Robbins and Williams Green 2017; Robbins 2020). While the penal substitution model of sin attributes a strong sense of moral culpability to the "sinner"—to the persons themselves—the *Christus victor* model of atonement found at churches like Pastor John's places the blame on these nonhuman spiritual others.

Further, this way of thinking about addiction as resulting from the interventions of malevolent spiritual others who can be driven out through prayer and deliverance challenges scholars to think beyond the framework of disciplined self-cultivation. Following Amira Mittermaier's (2012, 2011) analysis of the limits of the self-cultivation paradigm in relation to how Shaykh Qusi's followers understand some dreams to be acts of divine intervention, in this chapter and the one that follows we aim to open the anthropology of ethics to a deeper analysis of the place of relationality and the "role of an Elsewhere" in ethical life. Mittermaier draws on Godfrey Lienhardt's (1961) notion of an ethics of passion in an effort to illuminate an "ethics of relationality, one that recognizes that humans are always embedded in webs of relationships" (2012, 249). She writes that "the ethics of passion that emerges from my interlocutors' dream stories not only undoes the notion of a unified subject but also draws attention to the role of an Elsewhere in constituting the subject, and with it to elements of unpredictability and contingency" (249).

While such a perspective on personhood resonates with the works in African studies that we discussed earlier in this chapter, most of these works do not take ethics as their focus. One exception to this is Michael Lambek, whose work on ethics has questioned the priority Western thinkers have given to a "pure and unitary state of mind" as "the necessary source of ethical action and commitment"

(2010, 722). In exploring forms of ethics founded on a more "porous, passionable, or relational self" (729), Lambek breaks down moralized dichotomies between reason and passion and between the mind and the body. Like Mittermaier and Lambek's interlocutors, Daniella's life was shaped through a dialogue with beings eclipsed by the boundaries of secular thought. As will be true for those you will meet in the following chapter on spirit possession, Daniella interpreted her dreams as coming from an "Elsewhere," as messages (*obubaka*), as instructions to be interpreted carefully and taken seriously.[4]

In our efforts to understand the effects of receiving a message from God in a dream or of experiencing the embodied sensation of being delivered from a spirit, we are also moving away from an effort to understand what causes believers to hear God speaking to them and toward an effort to understand what hearing God *does* in their lives. By contrast, we might think about the way Tanya Luhrmann approaches both miraculous and mundane moments of hearing God's voice in her widely read book *When God Talks Back* (2012). In this book, Luhrmann argues that members of the Vineyard churches she studied in Chicago and California come to hear the voice of God through an engagement with a series of imaginative practices, or "cultural kindling," which cause them not only to have unusual sensory experiences more often but also to interpret these experiences as spiritually significant (see also Cassaniti and Luhrmann 2014). In contrast to Luhrmann, in this chapter we focus less on explaining the origins of Daniella's spiritual experiences and instead seek to describe these experiences as she and others at Pastor John's church did. We have asked not why these things occur, but what effects these experiences had in their lives going forward. This stance shifts our focus away from exploring the causes that might lead to the effect of a spiritual experience, and instead opens up space to explore how these experiences figure in processes of ethical-moral transformation.

DELIVERANCE

As we talked with Daniella on that first cool morning at Pastor John's, we could hear the voices of others scattered about the hall, talking in small groups. Some were talking quietly, but in the back, there was a man who was speaking loudly and sharply to a woman as he put his hands on her head. Every once in a while, her body jerked and rolled as his speech became punctuated with loud shouts.

Noticing this pair and wondering about this scene of what looked to her like what she imagined when she heard the word deliverance, China asked, "I hope this question doesn't offend you, but there is something I am wondering about that I hope you can help me with. Behind you, there's a man that has been praying for a woman. He is speaking very sharply, and she is shaking and making noises. What is that all about? Is it related to what we are talking about, or is it something different?"

"It is related, and it's called deliverance. That man is trying to cast a spirit out. The spirit is shouting for it is being sent out of its home and it is fighting to remain within the woman."

"Did people do that to you when you were being prayed for?" China asked.

"They did. There was a time when I even jumped off my chair. And the pastor doesn't need to touch you. When the place is filled with the Holy Spirit, when God's presence is there, you will see people jumping, yelling, making noise, because God is working on them. Those kinds of things stopped for me after the dream, but that doesn't mean that I stopped being delivered. . . . Deliverance is a process. It is not a one-day thing. It's a process where you go to God and confess your sins. First of all, you have to accept that you are a sinner. You have to confess to whatever led you into that curse. Or you may not have sinned, but your parents might have done something that brought that curse. Or your heart may be dirty, filled with bitterness, anger, and worry. . . . The Bible says, 'If my people called by my name confess their sins, I will hear from heaven and heal their land.'"

As Daniella puts it here, deliverance is not a one-day thing. Battles on the spiritual plane are processes that can involve years of repentance, prayer and fasting—a slow sedimentation of sacrifice. Furthermore, while her drinking was not necessarily something she could be held accountable for, she had to search her history for the sinful actions that might have opened her life to the spirits that had caused her problem drinking. Importantly, the history that she needed to access was not hers alone. Within this deeply relational conception of spiritual warfare, one's life can be opened to curses and the actions of spirits by the actions of family members, friends, or people with whom one has sexual relations. The possibility that one's life and one's salvation could be influenced by the actions of others whose sins could open a whole network of people to Satanic influence has sometimes led people to attempt to break ties with their extended families (Meyer 1998), but more often it leads to efforts to pray for the healing of the whole family as an unbreakable totality.

In addition, during the early stages of this process, before her experience of deliverance, Daniella continued to drink heavily. She was preparing herself in other ways, but sobriety was not a requirement. While relapses are expected in AA, people are also expected to leave alcohol behind right at the beginning of their effort to change. In contrast, following the logic of spiritual warfare Daniella could not be expected to stop drinking without deliverance, as the drinking was literally not under her control. There is also, again in contrast to AA, a radical break that separates a person from the possibility of relapse that takes place at the moment of deliverance. In AA, someone who has been sober for twenty years is thought to be as likely to relapse as someone who has been sober for a day. At Pastor John's, once a person is delivered, they are thought to be free of the thing that was causing them to drink. They are now fundamentally different from how they had been prior to the moment of deliverance. Those who have been delivered must still work to live righteously so as to avoid any activities that might re-invite demons into their lives. They must fill their hearts with the Holy Spirit so that the demon, if it tries to return, will not find a spiritual vacuum where it can easily take up residence again. All must be vigilant, making addiction no different from the other maladies that bring people to the church's crowded taxi stage.

RICHARD

On a cold rainy morning in May 2018, Sarah went back to Pastor John's to pay a visit to one of the other people whom we had come to know at the fellowship. It had been a few weeks since Sarah had last seen Richard, but she had heard someone say that he had been assigned to manage the parking lot. Sarah set off by *boda boda*, and by the time she reached Pastor John's the rain had stopped and the sun was strong. Since it was a public holiday, the parking lot was already full of cars despite the early hour. Over the tops of the cars, Sarah could see Richard, looking even thinner than he really was in his long green jacket, army boots, pale blue trousers, and a faded black t-shirt under the jacket. As he caught sight of her, Richard smiled broadly. "Praise God! Who told you that I am here in the parking?" Fumbling with his large black registration book and pen, he tried to find a chair where Sarah could sit. She refused the seat and so instead he handed her the black counter book and blue pen he was using to register the cars. "Sarah, today, it's you registering. Thanks for coming," he said with a smile as he jogged off to give instructions to one of the other men he was working with.

Left with the book and pen, Sarah tried to follow what she had seen him doing. A car came in and she noted down its license plate number, the owner's contact number, and gave the owner a card to be returned when coming to collect the car. Much to Sarah's relief, Richard soon returned and took back his book. Unlike Sarah, who was new on the job, Richard interacted freely and happily with all the people coming in to park their cars. Some were extremely friendly, and it was clear that they had become attached to him. Children came by and Richard played with them, giving one small boy some money to buy lunch. It was growing hot, and Richard persuaded Sarah to sit next to him in the shade. He gave her a mango. From time to time, cars came in and Richard jumped up to register them.

"This seems like a hard job, being out here from morning until late," Sarah said.

"Yes, but I have to serve the Lord," said Richard. "It is through service and humility that he helps me. You never know, sometimes I even get what I never expected. I've made a lot of friends, some tip me. Recently, I've even met a lady who works at Makerere University. She promised to get me forms so that I can go back to school on a government sponsorship. We are now planning for the 2020 intake."

Richard went on to explain that on Wednesdays he leaves from Pastor John's to go directly to another church on the other side of Kampala. There he sleeps a few hours and then gets up early in the morning to join in their door-to-door preaching ministry. "I believe God is training me for something big in ministry, for I teach the congregants and pray with them. Then afterwards I come back here and resume my work at the parking." As he talked, Sarah was sweating. It had become extremely hot and neither of them had any water to drink. Their conversation was also punctuated by cars coming in and out. One car broke down while it was coming in and Richard had to help push it.

"Seems you barely get free time these days," Sarah said. "Do you still get any time to learn from the teachings in the church? Or have you surpassed them now?"

"No," Richard said laughing. "Of course, I still attend. I usually attend the night ones. Those teachings are very helpful. I wouldn't have been what I am today without them. I used to try to do everything on my own, but I failed. Now I just listen, serve, and all is well."

On that morning in the parking lot, Richard had been sober for two years and had been living at the church for the better part of that time. Richard grew up in a family of distillers in a village in Central Uganda. He started drinking tonto when he was only seven and shifted to waragi and marijuana when he was fifteen, which he attributes to a sense of loneliness and isolation after his mother died when he was ten. Richard also started singing, and as he looks and sounds almost exactly like the Ugandan pop star—and now internationally-known politician—Bobi Wine, he found it easy to move through the clubs and ghettos of Kampala.

Richard first came to Pastor John's church in 2011. He had woken up to smoke but instead followed the music to the church. He continued to drink and smoke marijuana, but despite his substance use, he was embraced by the pastors, easily moving between church and ghetto. He eventually stopped smoking and drinking for seven months by moving onto the church property but started using again when a friend in the church, who was also still using, took him back to the ghetto over the weekend. Five years passed during which he wanted nothing to do with church. During this period of his life, he also spent seven months in the compound of a spirit medium, but eventually stole the money from the basket of offerings in the shrine and escaped.

On New Year's Eve 2016, as he was just about to enter a club to perform with some friends, Richard heard God tell him to throw down his cigarettes and marijuana and get born again. He didn't perform that night, but instead went to a crusade that was happening nearby to get saved. A month later he returned to Pastor John's church and has been living on the property, and been sober, ever since.

As is true for others attempting to move beyond alcohol by taking up residence at Pastor John's church, Richard has been given a series of small jobs with increasing levels of responsibility and visibility, the job in the parking lot being the most recent. While this job checking license plates might not seem like a big deal, this opportunity has given Richard a chance to interact with all the car-owning people who come to Pastor John's church. These people have come to admire Richard's positive attitude and the new system he developed for registering the plates and organizing the cars. This small job has given Richard a way of proving his trust-worthiness over a long period of time. It has also provided a means for him to increase his visibility to, and relationships with, others who might be able to offer a pathway toward other opportunities. And such connections seemed to be a vital part of his recovery process.

For Richard, then, Pastor John's was both the physical place where jobs and opportunities manifested themselves as well as the source of his belief that God is training him for something big. Together, these orient him toward this work and toward his future. Rather than feeling stuck in a difficult low-status job, far from the central action of the church office, Richard sees his work in the parking lot as a step on a divinely given pathway that is leading him to bigger and better things. While Richard is naturally a friendly, hardworking man, his hope that blessings would come to him through his work at the church changed the way he interacted with people and approached his work. This sense of possibility and hope probably made such blessings even more likely to come his way.

RADICAL HOPES

In his book *Radical Hope* (2006), the philosopher Jonathan Lear writes about the process through which the Crow chief Plenty Coups found the ability to respond to a situation of near total cultural collapse with what Lear calls "radical hope." "What makes this hope *radical*," Lear explains, "is that it is directed toward a future good-ness that transcends the current ability to understand what [the goodness] is" (103). In Lear's book, radical hope is what ultimately allowed Plenty Coups to stretch the Crow virtue of courage in a way that enabled him to face up to the reality of cata-strophic loss and to lead his people through it. While the importance of Lear's book is often framed in terms of the relevance of this type of hope when thinking about other situations of pending cultural collapse, here we want to attend to the *means* through which Plenty Coups managed to acquire the hope necessary to face, and cross over, this abyss and its relation to Richard and Daniella's stories.

In Lear's account, Plenty Coups acquires his radical hope through his reception of prophetic dreams. These dreams, the most important of which occurred when he was only nine or ten, warned him of the coming collapse of his way of life; confirmed that God's divine promise to the Crow would be sustained; and gave him direction about how to move forward through this collapse. Lear argues that these prophetic dreams, which became significant due to Plenty Coups's belief in their divine sanction, gave him the psychological resources he needed to avoid despair and allowed him to respond to the events that followed with remarkable creativity and courage.

While standing at the ethical abyss of sobriety differs in important ways from the abyss of civilizational collapse that Plenty Coups faced, stepping into any life that fundamentally differs from the life one has been living requires tremendous hope and courage. While we want to avoid stretching Lear's concept of radical hope beyond its limits, the means through which Daniella and Richard acquired the hope necessary to reach out toward new forms of life has striking similarities to what Lear describes. Like Plenty Coups, their hopes were founded on experiences of divine guidance. These experiences assured them of their place in God's plan and of the divine warrant for the difficult actions they would later undertake. Like Lear, we can be agnostic about the source of these experiences while still acknowledging the crucial role that dreams, words, visions, and embodied experiences played in their ethical lives. At one level, we can think of these experiences as giving them the psychological resources necessary to do what they did.

Joel Robbins's (2020) discussion of Christian theologies of interruption takes us one step closer to the emic terms that have been used by other Christians to think about these radical, hope-filled experiences of transformation. For Robbins and the theologians he engages, Christian interruptions both confront a person with an existential threat and promise that one will be returned to an enhanced continuity of life. In addressing his earlier writings on the conversion of the Urapmin in Papua New Guinea, Robbins brings together theological writings on interruption with his earlier arguments about the threatening prospects of non-being that the Urapmin collectively faced as the world around them began to shift through processes of colonialism and missionization. While the endangered ritual prestige that threatened the Urapmin is different from the threat posed by the experiences of despair and isolation that confronted Richard and Daniella in their addictions, there is a similar sense of an existential threat serving as the ground upon which God's interruption worked. The aim of this latter interruption, God's interruption, is not return, but newness, or rather a restoration to being the person that God originally created. Further, as Robbins discusses in a later chapter on passivity, such an interruption is not the result of the person's own efforts but is the effect of God's action in the world (see Scherz 2018a).

As Robbins notes, this way of thinking about transformation is quite different from many other ways of thinking about trauma as something which requires a slow and perhaps unending process of rebuilding. This contrast is crucial to Robbins's project, as he is committed to a form of anthropology that asks how our models of and for the world shape our experiences. In thinking about interruption in relation to trauma, Robbins is asking what difference it might make for people experiencing situations in which their very being seems to be at stake if they have a theory of that situation that gives them reason to hope that they will be restored to an enhanced continuity with the self they are meant to be.

As is clear in Richard and Daniella's stories, this hope extends well beyond the perceptions of a given individual. Richard's faith that God is "preparing him for something big" certainly gave him the energy he needed to face the many long scorching afternoons he spent in the parking lot, but the hope that his fellow church members had in the possibility that he was fundamentally separable from the spiritual forces that had caused him to drink also played a critical role in transforming his life. The same was true for Daniella. Nearly two years after being delivered, Daniella started serving at the church by voluntarily checking people's bags. She did this diligently for over two months from Monday to Saturday, and then was given an opportunity to work at the church radio. While she did not have any training in radio presenting, she was asked to present an early morning program. At first, this work was voluntary. The church was just beginning the radio programs and had no money to support this ministry, but after a while leadership began giving her an allowance. Since she stopped drinking, her relationship with her family has also been restored. A few months after she stopped drinking, she began staying at the home of one of her sisters on the weekends, often babysitting for her sister's children when she was there. Her father is also happy about her transformation. She has found many new friends through church, though she is not close to many of them. Among those she has come to know through the church was a man whom she met at a church-organized singles gathering in August 2018. The two married five months later and celebrated the marriage with a reception at a five-star hotel in grand style.

The early months of Daniella's marriage were somewhat difficult for her, as she adjusted to the work required to manage a home and a husband with the scrupulous attention to detail expected in many Ugandan families. During these first months she stopped her work at the radio station, and while she did not return to drinking, she found herself frustrated with the isolation of staying at home. She and her husband were also stressed by the financial pressures that followed the production of such an extravagant wedding. But time passed, and in the years that followed she was able to resume her work at the radio station and at the main reception desk at the church. She continues to describe this work and her physical presence in the space where she was healed as an important part of her life after alcohol, and she continues to pray and to attend to the ways that God is acting in her life. She also cares for her deceased sister's children. While this is a major responsibility, it is one she has taken on with joy, and these children are now a vital part of her life.

Richard has also continued with his work in the church since we first met him there in the parking lot, eventually rising in the ranks of those who work as ushers to the point where he has his own assistant. He also met a woman while working in the parking lot, and the two married in 2019. To Richard's great disappointment, however, she left him just weeks after the wedding. She had money and a job, and Richard suspects that she was disappointed by his relative poverty and limited ability to provide the sort of lifestyle to which she was accustomed. Her departure pushed Richard into a deep depression, and he even began to doubt God, but he continued going to church and his friends there encouraged him.

During the COVID-19 pandemic in 2020, a member of the church gave him a job overseeing construction projects at his home and gave him a place to stay and land where he could grow food. Unfortunately, he accidentally sprayed herbicide on the corn and cabbage he had planted, withering his entire crop. But the neighbors helped him with food, and he continued on. He began singing again, writing songs praising the goodness of God in his life, and hoping that maybe God would help him to return to his life as a musician. After the COVID-19 lockdowns ended, he began making recordings that could be played on the radio. On New Year's Eve 2023, he was one of the featured performers at the all-night celebrations that took place at Pastor John's church. He took to the stage in front of a crowd that could have filled three football fields and sang.

. . .

Despite the links between some forms of Protestantism and Alcoholics Anonymous (Brandes 2002; Antze 1987), the *Christus victor* model of recovery that shaped Richard and Daniella's experiences differs profoundly from that found in the inpatient recovery centers and recovery communities described in chapter 2 in terms of their relationships to their pasts, their futures, and to other people. Had they made their way to one of Kampala's newly founded AA groups, they would have been taught to see themselves as having a fundamental and unchanging condition. They would have learned to identify as addicts, as a particular kind of person (Hacking 1986). By contrast, at Pastor John's they and their fellow church members came to understand them as having been delivered from demonic spirits and born again, freed of the influence of forces that were never "them" anyway. The dense sociality of the church gave them the opportunity to demonstrate to others just how true this was as they spent their days working in the parking lot, the security desk, and the radio booth. By contrast, Kampala's addiction treatment centers all subscribe to the model of addiction as a chronic relapsing brain disease and deploy this model in ways that inadvertently foster forms of suspicion and hopelessness. In turn, these can make trusting relationships and forward movement difficult to achieve. While there are certainly tensions at Pastor John's as well, we argue that the possibility of seeing a person's past actions as authored by an Other allows people to form different kinds of relationships in the present and to live with a sense of confidence about what may be coming in the future. What we hope to have made clear in this chapter is that Daniella and Richard's spiritual experiences, and the ties of social connection that were made possible by a shared model of atonement in which their drinking was not entirely their own, gave them both a profound sense of hope that a new life was possible, and a safe and concrete space where that new life could take shape.

Yet, while the pastors we describe in this chapter and the mediums who we describe in the following one all seek to heal people through the ritual mediation of their relationships, their exposedness, their permeability, and their dividuality, they sharply disagree about the moral valence of the spiritual forces, the intangible persons, with whom people might be in relation. In this sense, there is both a degree of continuity between the church and the shrine as well as a profound sense of rupture.

5

Call and Response

Responding to Spirits in Kampala's Shrines

SEMUJU

It is Sunday evening and George is back again at Jjajja Kasumba's compound. It is a full house tonight, but George manages to find a seat on an old tire at the back of the compound where two of Jjajja Kasumba's assistants are playing Ludo. The game goes on for a long time and as the sky grows dark they ask George to hold a flashlight for them so that they can see. The dice clack against the handmade glass-topped board. There is a woman sitting next to George on the sagging tire and smoking a mixture of tobacco and herbs in a long *emindi* pipe, the smoke blowing into George's face as it makes its way up for the *balubaale* to enjoy. As she smokes, she spits into a small tin, which she periodically empties into the trench behind them. Some of this spit spills onto Ddungu, the dog, named for the lubaale of hunting, and she jokingly apologizes to him. Aunt Irene is also there, sewing beads onto leather sandals and selling twists of tobacco and small plastic bottles of waragi.

Though his back is getting sore from sitting, George continues to wait. Semuju, the young man he met there a few weeks before who struggled with drinking before finding Jjajja Kasumba, has promised to meet him, and George doesn't want to miss him. Finally, George's phone rings. It is Semuju. "Could you come and meet me? I'm just near the church. But hurry, I've left the baby sleeping alone in the house."

When George finds him, Semuju is standing near a small church, his slim frame barely visible in the dark. As he uses his flashlight to lead George along the road-side trenches, Semuju explains that he has been caring for his eighteen-month-old daughter for more than a year. The mother of the child left Semuju when he suggested that they consult a diviner to determine the cause of their financial problems. She accused him of being a witch and left—refusing to take the baby with

93

her. In the early days Semuju, a builder by trade, took the child to his jobs on construction sites, tying her onto his back as he worked.

This wife was also a heavy drinker, and he feared that one day she would come back and try to steal the child from the house. He had also come to believe that the balubaale took her away from him to prevent other marital problems in his life, despite the difficulty of caring for the baby alone. Semuju's own history with alcohol, and the role that his involvements with the balubaale played in ending it, are the reasons that George has come to find him.

Over the course of many more conversations, Semuju will tell George that he realized that he wasn't living a normal life when he was fifteen years old. His schooling was a problem because he could not see what was written on the chalkboard in his classroom. He had also begun to drink heavily, often taking a small bottle to be filled at an informal waragi distillery near his home, lying to the distillers and saying that he had been sent by his father. His uncles urged his father to attend to the balubaale spirits who they believed lay behind his drinking, to give them the care and attention that was their due, but at the urging of his stepmother his father refused to address the problem.

Semuju ultimately left home and went to live with a distant relative in Kampala. This relative, Jjajja Kasumba, is the leader of a community of people who participate in the form of mediumship and worship known in Uganda as *kusamira*. While Semuju was glad to find a home away from his stepmother, he was still drinking, fighting in bars, and getting fired from every job he found.

One day, while he was riding his bicycle, Semuju got into an accident. During the long period of convalescence that followed the accident, Semuju started questioning himself about his life and where his problems were coming from. He consulted Jjajja Kasumba, who began to counsel Semuju about his drinking and its spiritual causes.

With the help of the balubaale spirits who possess him during divinations, Jjajja Kasumba used *omweso* divination to consult with Semuju's ancestral spirits to discover the source of the problem. The spirits explained that Semuju had two opposing balubaale in him, Kiwanuka and Bamweyana. While Kiwanuka is a very good and powerful spirit who does not drink, Kiwanuka had sent another spirit, Bamweyana, to make Semuju drink in ways that would ruin his life to punish him for his neglect. The spirits said that Semuju must satisfy both Bamweyana, by making an offering of alcohol, and Kiwanuka by assembling a kit for him including a long white *kanzu*, a piece of bark cloth, a gourd, a stick, and a bag with money. Through these dual efforts, Semuju could effectively be relieved of Bamweyana's negative influences and come into a beneficial relationship with Kiwanuka.

After a long delay and many other signs, Semuju eventually relented and followed the instructions that the spirits had given him. He bought the necessary things and began to look for further instructions in his dreams. Soon after assembling the kit, Semuju stopped drinking and other things in his life began to change as well. Family members with whom he had lost touch resurfaced in truly miraculous ways, and he received an offer to work on a lucrative job in Juba in South Sudan, managing two trucks delivering agricultural supplies. Before leaving for Juba, Semuju left his lubaale kit with his best friend, instructing him to keep it well and agreeing to send him money each week in exchange for his help.

Things were fine for a while, but one morning the friend who was keeping the kit took the long white *kanzu* out of the bag and put it on. He also took the stick and used it to strike a sheep in Jjajja Kasumba's compound. The sheep died instantly. That same night, Semuju was sleeping with other Ugandans in a tent in Juba when he suddenly woke up craving tonto. Wondering if something had happened to his kit, Semuju called his wife in Kampala the next morning and told her to bathe with herbs and to check his kit to see if his friend had tampered with it. When she looked, she found that all of the money he had stored in the bag was gone.

Distraught and late to work, Semuju got dressed and went where the trucks were offloading the daily shipment from Kampala. As soon as he arrived, one of the truck owners told him that he didn't need him anymore; he had gotten someone else. Then another called to give him the same news. Semuju was suddenly and inexplicably jobless. He called Jjajja Kasumba for help. When he heard the story, Jjajja Kasumba went and questioned the friend who had been keeping the kit and chased him from the compound.

With no job, Semuju decided to return to Uganda. Before boarding the bus home, he used all of his remaining money to buy tot packs of waragi, stuffing every pocket of his baggy trousers with plastic sachets. When he reached Kampala, he was drunk and nearly unconscious. In the week that followed, Semuju drank with abandon. Luckily, someone recognized him one night passed out on the side of the road and carried him back to Jjajja Kasumba's compound.

Eventually Semuju was able to reassemble the kit, and once he did, he was able to stop drinking. This was in 2012, and ever since he has not had any problems with alcohol. He makes sure to keep the gourds he has left for Bamweyana filled with beer and regularly lights fires for Kiwanuka. He has also started to take up the necessary training to become a *ssenkulu mandwa*, an advanced level of initiation in the community. From time to time, he drinks a little beer or a little tonto, but only during rituals or other offerings; it never causes him any difficulties now that he has again settled his problems with Kiwanuka and Bamweyana.

· · ·

In this chapter, we build on the argument we made in chapter 4 concerning the affordances of spiritual experiences, relational models of personhood, and the importance of social connections in processes of ethical transformation. As in the preceding chapter, Semuju's story speaks to the benefits of experiencing oneself as living in a world that is densely populated by beings that might be obscured in certain versions of medical, social science, and philosophical discourse. While the experiences of people like Daniella and Semuju differ radically in terms of how they understand the moral valence of the spirits that possessed them and whether these spirits were to be exorcised through deliverance or embraced and accommodated, they both found themselves called to respond to forces that seemed to come from beyond themselves. The members of Pastor John's church believe that many maladies are caused by the invasion of an "extraordinary, harmful, abnormal presence" (de Heusch 1981, 155) that must be exorcised through deliverance. By contrast, in the forms of possession found at shrines like the one led by Jjajja Kasumba, "the alien presence is no longer considered to be a pathological state but rather a pure epiphany. Far from being rejected as an evil, the spirit is accepted as a blessing" (156). Here "the purpose of initiation is not to expel the god, to exorcise him as in inauthentic, undesirable possession, but instead to accept him, to accommodate oneself to him, to deliver oneself up, body and soul, to him after learning how to do so" (159).

In this chapter, we explore this path of acceptance and accommodation by focusing on the dynamics of responsivity and ritual in the lives of people who gather around Jjajja Kasumba and his *ssabo* (shrine).[1] While we might read some of the activities that take place around the ssabo as acts of promising to commit oneself to a new kind of life (Lambek 2015), such as the moments when Semuju constructed and then reconstructed the kit of Kiwanuka's things, perhaps it is akin to the moment of commitment played out in the ingestion of the herbal emetic therapies described in chapter 3. Yet such a reading would, in this case, fundamentally misread Semuju's relationship to Kiwanuka. To understand this situation correctly, we must remember that the drinking was not the violation that Kiwanuka was punishing. Instead, the drinking was the punishment that Kiwanuka was inflicting on account of Semuju's failure to keep his ancestral covenant. In assembling the kit, Semuju was acknowledging and attending to promises and covenants between his ancestors and Kiwanuka that long precede his existence.

Understanding this situation, and many others like it, requires us to understand how people engage not only with the criteria established by the promises they make but also, and perhaps more importantly, how people find themselves caught up in situations defined by criteria and relationships that precede their own existence. It was only by acting in accordance with the demands of these prior relationships that Semuju found reason to hope that Kiwanuka would keep his promise to bless his life and to cease his punishment. Drawing on phenomenological writings in both anthropology and philosophy that explore these dynamics of responsivity and responsibility (Waldenfels 2011; Mattingly et al. 2017; Schwarz Wentzer 2014; Dyring and Grøn 2021; Zigon 2007, 2018, 2021; Mattingly 2018; Leistle 2014, 2016; Ingold 2017; Gunther 2006; Throop 2018) we ask how our thinking about the ethical life might differ if we foregrounded prior entanglements and forms of dependence that exceed our willing commitments. Anthropological understandings of ethics are so often founded upon an understanding of the subject as acting from a position of relative freedom (Laidlaw 2002). What would happen if, instead of seeing ethics as an activity engaged in from a position of relative freedom, we looked more carefully at the prior entanglements that demand our response? And perhaps more importantly, how might a decision to respond transform a person's experience of the world and its possibility?

EMPEWO

Jjajja Kasumba's ssabo lies at the bottom of a steep dirt path just off one of the main roads in one of Kampala's southern neighborhoods. Near the bottom of the hill, there is a small opening in a wall of lush green vines. Next to this opening is a large *mutuba* tree, the tree used for making bark cloth, filled with the small spherical nests of yellow weaver birds. Stooping down to pass through the tunnel of vines, you enter the compound of round, brick, tin-roofed huts. Around the compound there are several fires burning, and the strange flat-smelling smoke of burning dung and herbs hangs in the air. Along the side wall of the compound is a long wooden bench where women are often seated, smoking herbs and tobacco in their long thin *emindi* pipes, sending pleasing puffs of smoke to the spirits.

Jjajja Kasumba's ssabo is a spacious and cool circular room with a high roof made of iron sheets. The roof of Kasumba's ssabo is held up by four smooth wooden poles. At the tops of the poles and all around the circumference of the roof are dry calabashes and bags coated in a thin layer of dusty soot. The floor of the ssabo is made of packed dirt and covered wall-to-wall by large mats made of different plastics and fibers in varying states of repair. In the far-left corner, toward the back, there is a square area covered with white animal hides surrounded by a row of thin iron spears with different kinds of points.

Jjajja Kasumba is a *musamize* (pl. *basamize*), or someone who has been initiated into the practice of mediumship and spirit possession through the ritual performance of kusamira. He is also a *ssenkulu mandwa*, meaning that he has reached a very advanced level among those who have been initiated and is the leader of a community of basamize, or people who participate in this form of mediumship and worship.[2]

As a *ssenkulu mandwa*, Jjajja Kasumba is responsible for diagnosing the problems his clients face through a process of divination. As discussed in chapter 3, visiting a *ssenkulu mandwa* like Jjajja Kasumba is often a last resort in a therapeutic quest, typically prompted by the experience of a series of misfortunes for which the family can find no other explanation or solution. During omweso divination, Jjajja Kasumba invites the balubaale spirits who originally came to possess him through a prior, and now long passed, process of diagnosis and ritual to communicate with the spirits of the person who has come to consult. This spirit who possesses him will then speak through him and also via the arrangement of the cowrie shells, coins, and other objects that he will scatter and sweep with his hands. In this way the spirits will communicate what the problem is, what is causing the problem, and how it might need to be addressed.

While *omweso* divination sometimes reveals the cause of the problem to be witchcraft (*okuloga*) or simply the result of natural causes, a revelation that the problem is connected to balubaale may be followed by the performance of kusamira. Kusamira, which is also the verb for praying in Luganda and several related languages, refers to a set of practices aimed at a collective production and reproduction of well-being and prosperity (Hoesing 2021). More specifically, it refers to the efforts made by the members of a patrilineal clan, now often in the company of a hired *ssenkulu mandwa* like Kasumba and his assistants, who use drums, gourd rattles, and singing to call the balubaale to come and speak to them by possessing one of the assembled clan members. The members of the clan must be assembled because the spirits to be addressed and welcomed are not spirits foreign to a person or family who have come and attacked from nowhere, but are rather spirits who have always been attached to the person and their kin. The demands that they make through illnesses and other problems are demands on the collective. They precede the existence of the person and speak to a set of relations and obligations that likewise preexisted the person's own beginning.

Immediately following kusamira, the family will organize a feast (*ekijjulo*) as a way of making an offering and satisfying the demands of the ancestors who have come during kusamira. At this feast, a goat will be sacrificed, and the liver and kidney burned along with sweet starchy *gonja* bananas. As with many medicines in Uganda and elsewhere, the names of plant medicines are linguistically linked to their purpose (Langwick 2010; Stroeken 2010). Here the word *gonja* is related to the verb *okugonjoola*, to solve problems—the solving of problems being precisely what the family aims to do by making this offering. Such a feast may also be delayed until a specified time in the future, at which time those assembled to perform kusamira expect that they will be able to use a portion of the wealth that has come by way of the blessings of the ancestors to make the necessary offerings.

Organizing a family to engage in kusamira is no small feat at a time when such practices are seen by many people in Uganda, nearly all of whom practice either Christianity or Islam, as spiritually dangerous or even Satanic. As discussed in the last chapter, contemporary Pentecostals like those who pray at Pastor John's church readily equate traditional religious practices with the forging of Satanic covenants (Meyer 1999), with some Pentecostals rejecting even the cultural practices accepted by Catholics, Anglicans, and Muslims, such as a groom giving a rooster to the brother of the bride. That said, even people who are not Pentecostal or intently focused on the spiritual dangers of traditional religious practices may fear to engage with balubaale in kusamira or even to visit a shrine like Jjajja Kasumba's with the intention of seeking out such an engagement. While part of this may stem from fears about what others might think or say, there is also a real sense of fear of what may unintentionally result from such involvements: that a relation with the spirits could be opened that could not easily be ended or closed and that the demands that such a relationship might impose could quickly become excessive.

With this in mind, we can see that finding the necessary funds to repair or reconstruct the family shrine and to pay for the event and the animal sacrifices is one thing, but assembling one's clansmen is entirely another. Given the expense and difficulty of organizing kusamira, many who have problems with balubaale may make more private sorts of offerings, such as the gourd (*endeku*) of tonto that one regular participant at Jjajja Kasumba's ssabo set out in a locked room of his home, secretly and out of sight of his staunchly religious Anglican family. Others might go alone or in the company of a few others to visit Tanda or other sacred sites to make offerings.

Yet, the gathering together of the family members can be crucial because the person or persons suffering from the misfortunes may not be the one the lubaale seeks to possess. For example, the demands of the lubaale may manifest in the infertility of a woman, but it may be her sister who will find herself possessed by the lubaale when the family gathers for kusamira and who may subsequently come into a deeper relationship with this spirit through a process of more intensive training. Once a spirit possesses a person, this person and all of their paternal relatives and clan members become basamize. Medical anthropologists working in Africa have long attended to the importance of social bonds in processes of healing, and the anthropological literature on spirit possession has gone a long way both to unsettle bounded visions of the self and to open readers to more porous and permeable understandings of personhood (Lambek 2010). Yet this conceptualization of the interconnectedness of clan members, the distribution of maladies and the production of well-being across bodies, and the necessity of the cooperation of kin in the process of healing pushes this even further.

While Jjajja Kasumba sometimes translated the word balubaale as "ancestors," in this context this term refers to something far more complex than the deceased members of a person's own lineage, something closer perhaps to what is sometimes termed "powers" or *empewo* (literally, winds). The spirits of specific deceased people (s. *muzimu*, pl. *mizimu*) may sometimes be addressed in these contexts, but far more common are engagements with other sorts of spirits. Among these are spirits who guard or assist other spirits or who can be sent to do particular kinds of work and are sometimes housed or kept by their owners in horns, as described in chapter 3 (s. *ejjembe*, pl. *amayembe*). They may also include spirits who existed before human beings and who are associated with specific natural places like trees, rocks, or wells, and can come in the form of an animal like a python or leopard (s. *musambwa*, pl. *misambwa*), and, perhaps most importantly, a pantheon of other named Kiganda spirits (s. *lubaale mandwa*, pl. *balubaale mandwa*). The same named spirit can also come in different forms, sometimes appearing as a *lubaale mandwa*, and sometimes as a *jjembe*. All of this said, while we have, for the sake of clarity, tried to offer a brief schematic here, in life the spirits appear less as members of classes or types than they do as particular persons with specific qualities, biographies, and relations to other spirits. One is unlikely to learn about them in a systematic way; rather, the spirits are learned as one encounters them in specific contexts, through embodied experience, performance, and narrative.

Each of these spirits has preferences and taboos dictating what sorts of food and drink they may consume; crucially for our purposes, only some drink alcohol. Many are also associated with natural phenomena. For example, Kiwanuka is associated with lightning and electricity and Mukasa with water, boats, and childbirth—especially the birth of twins. Their respective sacred sites are elaborately decorated with these features in mind. Kiwanuka's tree is filled with electrical cables and light bulbs, while Mukasa's is stacked with small wooden boats. Dreams featuring these elements can be taken as clear signs as to which spirit may be asking something from you. All of these powers are subordinate to Katonda, who is the creator of them all. While the Ugandan anthropologist and poet Okot p'Bitek (1971) has argued that both anthropologists and missionaries have misled readers through their efforts to emphasize the similarities between beings like Katonda and the God of Christianity, Jjajja Kasumba, who is himself a practicing Muslim, and the other basamize that we spoke with, were emphatic that Katonda, Allah, and the God of Christianity were one and the same and that the balubaale too were angels and saints called by other names (see Mbiti 1970).

At times these spirits may alight upon the heads of the basamize, but offerings can also take quieter forms, as we saw with Semuju's need to keep the kit he assembled for Kiwanuka safe from harm. Similarly, while balubaale may mount the heads of the basamize to speak directly, they also, and perhaps more often, send their messages in dreams.[3] Some of these dreams are interpreted to reveal advice and predictions about one's life, such as a student dreaming of a pile of white papers predicting their success on upcoming exams. In other cases, dreams sent by balubaale are read for signs about which of the balubaale are troubling the dreamer and what they are demanding in exchange for the dreamer's release from his problems.

Finally, while nearly any of these types of spirits may cause problems related to alcohol as a way of demanding the attention and care of those they visit, there is one specific lubaale, Bamweyana, who we have already met and who is worth mentioning by name. Bamweyana is one of the balubaale from the royal family of Buganda, and he is often sought out by those seeking to develop their musical talents or to close lucrative business deals. Many musicians in Uganda flock to his shrines, carrying calabashes of tonto and bags and hats woven from palm leaves to ask him to help them polish their talents. There, they drink and smoke freely as they sing and dance. He is also known for drinking. When other *empewo* wish to punish someone for their failure to attend to them properly, they will ask Bamu, as he is affectionately known, to drink through that person, as one drinks through a straw, until that drinking destroys the person's life to such a grave extent that they realize the importance of attending to the demands of the *empewo*.

RITUAL, CARE, AND SOCIALITY

What was perhaps most striking in the rituals we attended at Jjajja Kasumba's ssabo and in the moments of offering, feasting, and visiting that we witnessed at the other sacred sites where we spent time over the course of this work, were the ways that ritual engagements with spirits resembled other intimate human relationships of caregiving (Kopytoff 1971; Lambek 1981). To purchase Ndawula's favored gifts of fruits and honey and then to travel to Tanda[4] to place them among the other offerings in front of his iron spears, each topped with ten curving fingers making an Islamic gesture of prayer, is surely an act of sacrifice, but it is also an act of visiting, entirely akin to the act of purchasing bread, margarine, sugar, and washing soap on one's way to visit rural relatives.

While these relations with intangible persons like Ndawula are of crucial importance, the ssabo also offers a space for a new set of materially and affectively rich social relationships that do not center on drinking to emerge. To be clear, Jjajja Kasumba's compound is by no means a place where alcohol is unwelcome. In fact, the consumption of alcohol is an important part of the feasts offered to many of the spirits and also part of more everyday forms of sociality. That said, the ssabo is a space where people who cannot drink are respected and where not drinking can be understood as evidence of their being cared for by the balubaale. Further, and perhaps more importantly given the social losses that can follow a decision to leave the conviviality of the bar, it is a place where people can come together to socialize, the laughter of the Ludo games alternating with the sound of drum skins being tested and tightened as people prepare to care for the balubaale and to be cared for by them in return.

Even where kin may no longer be willing to participate in the performance of kusamira, the collective of the healer's compound proved itself to be a vital force of support as people attempted to rebuild their lives. This collective was comprised of people engaged in processes of spiritual healing from a wide range of maladies, most of whom were not related by blood. Their interactions with one another not only took place in the ritual settings of the *ekijjulo* offering and kusamira rituals, which they participated in on behalf of others who came to Jjajja Kasumba seeking help, but also occurred in a much more mundane way. Jjajja Kasumba's compound was not only a place for engaging the spirits. It was a place for chatting and playing Ludo. People talked with one another as they filled their long *emindi* pipes with tobacco and herbs to offer the smoke up to the balubaale. People traveled with one another as they went to help Jjajja Kasumba organize performances of kusamira for other families, and as they went with one another to visit the *misambwa* at sacred sites throughout the region.

Like the Pentecostals you met in the last chapter, who find their days and nights filled with cell meetings and overnight prayer sessions, choir practices, and church renovation projects, and who simply have a quasi-public space to go to when they don't want to be at home, the people who have come to Jjajja Kasumba to be healed find that they too have a new space and a new community apart from the bars they have left behind. While alcohol is not prohibited and may even be served at rituals where the spirits in attendance are ones who drink alcohol, this is also a space where people like Semuju are supported in their efforts to refrain from drinking, even as they may continue to socialize with people who do drink.

Crucially though, the sociality to be found at Jjajja Kasumba's is not to be found in human beings alone. While there is certainly the day-to-day social life of the Ludo games and casual talk, there are also more intensive moments of conviviality that intentionally seek to welcome the spiritual visitors who are also part of this community into the space of the shrine, to care for them and appreciate them through gifts of food and music and to receive their blessings and advice as they speak to and enjoy the experience of being together.

EKIJJULO

We had spent many afternoons sitting in the cool darkness of the ssabo with Jjajja Kasumba and his assistants before we were ever invited to participate in any collective rituals. For many long afternoons we would sit, chatting, folding, and refolding our knees from one side to another against the dusty surfaces of the mats as we all learned to trust each other, until finally Jjajja Kasumba invited us to contribute something for firewood and to come for the *ekijjulo* that was to be held that coming Sunday evening.

On the afternoon of the feast, we arrived around 5:00 p.m. While we suspected that the feast might begin much later than the slated 6:00 p.m. start time, we hoped that we might be able to chat with people before it started. But as we entered the compound, we were surprised to find that there was no one there, until we saw a large pile of old and new shoes heaped at the entrance to the ssabo. Sarah and China had lost track of George at this point, but someone told us to go inside, so we took off our shoes and went in.

It was dark inside, and it took our eyes some time to adjust to the dark and to the smoke. The place was full of people crammed together and we struggled to find a seat. It seemed that the drumming and singing had been in process for some time. Drummers were beating the drums, and Jjajja Kasumba was leading the call and response of the *balongo* songs. Among the drummers was a man whom we had seen become possessed by Kiwanuka as we sat around chatting in the compound some days earlier. Everyone, except for the drummers, sat on the ground, singing, and clapping in time with the drums. Everyone was still themselves.

As we found our seats and our eyes adjusted to the light, we could see a feast laid out on the floor at the center of the ssabo. A group of women and children were peeling a large pile of unpeeled steamed bananas (*mpogola*) that were lying in a pile on top of a large steamed banana leaf (*olujjuliro*). There were also small bits of meat and long stringy mushrooms.

When the women and children finished peeling, they began placing portions of whole and half bananas and small pieces of meat on torn banana leaves and serving them to the assembled guests. Some people did not take the food, George explained, because they were fasting for Ramadan.[5] China was handed a hot moist banana on a leaf with some small pieces of fat and meat. As we ate, the drumming and singing continued. When everyone was finished, the women serving gracefully cleared the remaining leaves and took them out to the compound. After the first meal, Jjajja Kasumba started a song, "*Agabudde n'abaana be*" (She has served her children).

As the center of the ssabo was cleared, the children were invited forward. First, Jjajja Kasumba's daughter, a slender girl of seven in a long Islamic dress and headscarf, tentatively started a *baakisimba*,[6] and then the other smaller children, boys and girls together, joined her to dance *baakisimba* in the center of the ssabo while everyone sang a song for the spiritual *balongo* (twins) Walumbe and Nambi (Kizza 2010).

Jjajja Kasumba later explained that because they have not been handled well, the *balongo* have blocked development all over the world. He said that it is often because of them that people fail to find jobs or school fees for their children. These problems can come not only from a failure to handle physical twins well, but also from a failure to handle the spiritual twins, the children of Katonda, well. He told us that the *balongo* feasts "release" quicker than any other feast.

The children danced beautifully. It was so tender how they danced, and everyone else sang and enjoyed them. We were all together, everyone playing their role in this performance perfectly, but without direction or tension. After the song finished, the children left the ssabo, and most of the people followed them bit by bit. The drummers hung their drums up and went out, telling us to come back for another feast, which is being cooked. We sat for a while in the smoky ssabo, not fully knowing what to do. Having heard Jjajja Kasumba ask the couple seated near us if they had the sesame seeds they had been asked to bring, George suggested that the man and woman seated next to China had organized the *balongo* feast.

George eventually moved out of the ssabo to stretch his legs. Sarah and China went out too, just to clear the smoke from their eyes. Outside the ssabo, the ladies were preparing food for the next feast. As we talked to the women, we could see Amos, Jjajja Kasumba's assistant, dressed in a bark cloth robe fastened at one shoulder over his trousers and polo shirt. He looked very handsome dressed like this.

Several years before, Amos had been working as a hawker, selling used shoes house-to-house with his friends. He was renting a room with one of these friends for 40,000 UGX per month, but they weren't making much money and soon fell behind on their rent. He owed his landlord four months' rent, and he couldn't get it from anywhere. He didn't have any capital left or any other job that he could do. He was always worried about getting money, and his fellow hawkers taught him to drink as a way of forgetting. "Alcohol was like a blanket that covered me during that hard time," he said.

Amos and his friend were eventually evicted from their room. They moved into a shack nearby and often had to skip meals. His friend's brother decided to rescue them with some money for rent. He gave them the money, but they ended up buying alcohol with it instead of using it to secure a new house. Amos says that by this time alcohol had become like fuel for him, and that if he missed a day of drinking, his body would become very weak. His health deteriorated and his lips became red.

When he couldn't hold it together anymore, he decided to go home to his village. In the village, Amos began to dream. Through these dreams he came to realize that his drinking was not only the result of the stress of poverty, but also a sign that his ancestral spirits were not happy and that there were rituals he would need to perform to settle them. Messages in his dreams led him to the exact location of Jjajja Kasumba's ssabo. Though he had never been there before, he arrived effortlessly. Jjajja Kasumba welcomed Amos with open arms and led him through the required rituals. To cool down the ancestral spirits, he had to buy bark cloth, a spear, and other things. Since making these offerings, Amos has found that if he tries to drink the waragi he used to love, he gets a bad pain in his stomach. He drinks beer occasionally, but never exceeds two bottles.

Since that time, Amos has also become one of Jjajja Kasumba's favorite apprentices and is presently a *mutende*, a person in training to become a *ssenkulu mandwa*. On this particular night, Amos was moving back and forth from the bathing area at the back of the compound around to the side of the ssabo and then going inside. Ahead of him each time was a heavy-set middle-aged man wearing only a new red printed cloth wrapped around himself. He was wet and had small bits of green leaves stuck to his body. They moved back and forth several times as we talked to the women.

The women explained to us that the next feast would be for the female spirits of the water. It would be held inside the ssabo because these spirits eat *matooke*. The ssabo is dedicated to the lubaale spirit Muwanga and *matooke* is also his food, so the ladies can also have their feast inside.

The children were playing as they waited for the next feast to start. They collected fallen nests from the weaver birds. First, they kicked them like balls. Then one put one over his hand like a boxing glove and others wore them as shoes. We were not sure what the offense was, but Jjajja Kasumba was not pleased by this. He came over and took the hand of one of the children very firmly in his hand; the child kneeled down as Jjajja Kasumba squeezed the child's hand and whispered to him very quietly but very firmly. Jjajja Kasumba returned to the shrine and the children stopped their game.

There was a sharp rattling coming from inside the shrine. George thought it might be a child playing with one of the rattles, but someone told us that the rattles were being shaken as wood was added to the fire inside the ssabo to invite the balubaale to come. The women checked the *matooke* and started to remove the leaves and stems that have been used for the steaming.

As we all moved back into the ssabo to take our places, a man poured kerosene into a large glass lantern and lit the wick. It was around seven o'clock, and it was beginning to get dark. The lantern cast a glow, and we could see the dark outlines of the shields and spears set off by the fire behind them. This space, where we had now been many times before, was coming to life.

The drummers took their places, and Jjajja Kasumba started to sing the *balongo* songs in a strong resonant voice. "*Leka emmere yo tojjula, gyenva ndiddeyo-leka emmere yo tojjula lubaale anampa*," he sang: "Please do not serve me with your food; I have already eaten. Lubaale has given food to me." They sang call and response with everyone singing and clapping along with him. George knew some of the songs well and joined in.

The women who had been cooking now brought the enormous bundle of *matooke* and the smaller pouch of folded banana leaves that contained the steamed meat. They placed these on banana leaves spread on the floor at the center of the hut and began to unwrap them.

Aunt Irene was dancing. Until this moment, we had always known her as the kind middle-aged woman seated at the back of the compound, round and motherly, sewing beads on shoes and selling twists of tobacco for pipes. Her corner of the compound is home to the nightly Ludo game, and hours can pass as people play and joke with one another.

Now a soft-spoken woman in middle age, Aunt Irene drank heavily when she was in secondary school. She started out just taking a little for fun, but in 1991, when she was in her late teens, she had progressed to drinking crude waragi and dropped out of Senior Four before she completed her exams. She stopped working and went days without bathing.

Her family members were ashamed of her drinking, and several tried to counsel her. Her niece tried taking her to the church of a famous Pentecostal pastor in Kampala. But the niece soon disappeared and when she resurfaced, she was sick with HIV and died, so Irene decided to leave the church. Her paternal grandmother tried to help her with her drinking problem by giving her an herbal medicine to be taken with milk. After taking this, she stopped drinking for a short time, but soon started again. The fact that this medicine did not work was taken as a sign by her family that there were larger spiritual forces, *empewo*, that were making her drink.

While many members of Irene's family were Anglicans who refused to engage with traditional religious practices, others had already constructed an ancestral home, and Irene was taken directly there without the need to consult a healer outside of the family. Upon reaching the ancestral home, she felt at peace.

Soon after she arrived, the *musambwa* spirit Bamweyana possessed her elder brother. Through him, Bamweyana explained that she was possessed by the spirit of his wife, Nakayaga, and that Bamweyana was causing her to drink as a way of demanding her attention. He said that, as his wife, she needed to provide him with alcohol, shoes, baskets, spears, bark cloths, and other things. Even before this, she had dreamed of a mentally ill woman, which she later learned is a sign of both Nakayaga and Bamweyana. Without further guidance, she bought a calabash of tonto and a palm bag and shoes for Bamweyana. She stayed in the ancestral home for three weeks and continued to return from time to time after that, each time taking alcohol with her to offer to Bamweyana.

Once Irene began making these offerings, she gradually stopped drinking. "If a lubaale wants your attention, it will find ways to hurt you," she said. In her case, Bamweyana made her drink in ways that threatened to destroy her life, but once she recognized him through participation in rituals and making offerings to him, she was able to stop drinking.

Many people who noticed her change wondered and asked how she was able to overcome alcohol. Irene only told her secret to those who were closest to her. Many of her relatives did find out though, and, as they were Pentecostals, did not take this well. They knew that she had a problem but would have preferred that she went for prayers in the Christian church instead. While Irene says that prayers never helped her, she has remained an active member of an Anglican parish.

That night Irene was at the center of the ssabo. Her short fine braids, dyed red at the end, flew as she tossed her head backward and forward. She was wearing a pink short-sleeved shirt buttoned to just below her breasts over a brown tank top. She rolled her head back and forth and danced hard.

The drumming stopped, and Jjajja Kasumba asked her who the visitor is. In a high breathy voice, Irene told us that she was Nanseeko, a female lubaale *mandwa* associated with laughter. Jjajja Kasumba welcomed her and greeted her and the drumming resumed again.

Nanseeko, no longer Irene, went down on her knees with the other women who were serving. They too flung their heads back and forth as they danced on their hands and knees, arching their backs up and down.

Nanseeko began to laugh, talking quickly and helping the other women to serve the food as they all continued to dance on their hands and knees. The women put large portions of *matooke* and meat onto banana leaves and distributed them to everyone assembled in the ssabo. These portions were passed around, and people ate. One of the women serving the food raised a piece of meat to Sarah's mouth. Sarah tried to refuse, but the woman insisted and placed the food in her mouth. Sarah looked disgusted and elated at the same time. Then a different woman serving did the same to China. She lifted a large pinch of thin tube-like strands to China's mouth. China, not sure what they were, feared that they were tiny entrails of some sort. The woman placed them in China's mouth; she could not refuse. Then the women began to serve the soup. They took tiny cups folded from bits of banana leaf and dipped them into the *luwombo*, lifting the cups to the lips of those gathered to feed them the soup. One of the women lifted the cup to China's mouth, and it was salty and hot.

When everyone was done, the banana leaves and leftovers were cleared and taken outside. Throughout the feasting, the singing and drumming continued. As the women returned from the work of clearing the leaves, the drumming picked up, and the singing became more focused. It was now completely dark outside, but the inside of the ssabo glowed in the light of the the fire and the lantern. The beam of a battery-operated headlamp worn by one of the women dancing flashed across the space as she moved her head to the music.

The women who had been serving along with Irene were all clearly possessed now. They took water from clay pots with long narrow necks into their mouths and then sprayed the water over us as they and we danced; big sprays of water showered over the dancing crowd. Water hit our faces, splashing in our eyes and soaking our clothes. These are blessings, but they are also fun, rowdy, and playful.

As the drummers started a new song, the women possessed by the female spirits of the lake sat down on the floor, each in the lap of the one behind. They placed the children, up to maybe seven years old, and including babies, some of whom were crying, between themselves. The women started to rock side to side together; they were clearly in a boat paddling across the water. The drummers drummed and we continued to clap and sing. China and Sarah bent their knees softly, and shook their hips, letting the weight of their bodies do the shaking, feeling the freedom of the fat and flesh moving itself.

The song shifted and the women got out of their boat. The oldest of the women was now a mother, Nagadya, cradling adults in her arms, as they made their requests. She took Sarah first, holding her in her lap. Then many others came. She cradled them, embracing them, squeezing them, and shaking them. Her gestures were quick and strange, her eyes no longer quite in this world. After she finished with each, she took their hands and blew softly and quickly on their palms.

China sat in her lap too. Nagadya asked her if she wants money; China said that she doesn't, she wants peace and happiness. *Mirembe, Sanyu.* This is true. These are the things she feels are missing in herself some of the time. She wants to be less restless.

Shortly after she finished with China, the woman possessed by Nagadya beat her chest twice with both hands and then lifted her hands in the air, a gesture that means she was leaving. She was going. The woman was back to herself. She calmed almost instantly. Her movements became more fluid, and her eyes refocused.

Irene now returned to the center of the floor and began to dance more intensely, and those around her sang energetically with the drummers. As she danced, she moved to the fire near the entrance of the ssabo and stepped into the burning coals. When she returned to the center of the ssabo, she got down on her hands and knees and danced, arching her back and throwing her head up and down so that her hair flew back and forth.

Jjajja Kasumba reached behind himself for a large bark cloth. He threw the bark cloth over Irene as she danced on her knees, covering her completely as she continued to dance under the cloth. After a minute, she sat back, wrapping the cloth loosely around her head and body, covering herself completely. From inside the cloth, she spoke in the same high voice as before, now identifying herself as Nakayima. Jjajja Kasumba addressed her very kindly and directly. As they talked, the drumming stopped, and the ssabo was silent except for their voices. Jjajja Kasumba spoke to Nakayima with a sort of care and respect that anyone would wish to receive. She was treated as an honored visitor. He thanked her for coming, and asked if she drinks juice (*mubisi*) or alcohol (*omwenge*); she said that she takes *mbide* juice (juice also used to brew tonto). He asked her to make it possible for him to travel to Mecca. After a few minutes of talking like this, the drummers started again, and Nakayima returned to dancing under the cloth on her hands and knees. She moved up and down, rapidly arching her back and head in time to the beat of the drums. We all sang and clapped.

After some time, Nakayima returned to sitting with the bark cloth wrapped around her head, talking with Jjajja. Then she danced again. Eventually the bark cloth came off, and Irene returned to herself. Shortly after Irene became Irene again, the other women who had been possessed came back to themselves as well and complained that they had just arrived, and no one had given them any food. Jjajja Kasumba interjected that some food has been saved, and he produced a large portion that he kept back. Irene sat down in the center of the ssabo and ate ravenously. Jjajja Kasumba gently asked her to move to one side so that the drumming could continue.

One of the drummers came away from the drums and stood tall at the edge of the circle. He began to dance; he was now Kiwanuka. George whispered to China that he was Kiwanuka in *jjembe* form, the strongest of all the forms, and translated: he was saying that he wanted even to climb the poles. He danced energetically, springing up and crouching down low.

Another older woman in a *gomesa* with short braids became possessed again at the same time. She danced *baakisimba* while on her knees; they were both dancing, then they sat next to each other. A basket was placed in front of each of them, and people placed banknotes in the baskets. The baskets were evened. People greeted them, and we too came forward and knelt to greet them.

As the drumming continued, Jjajja Kasumba came to the center of the floor. He yanked one of the spears near the fireplace out of the ground, took the enormous *lubugo* (bark cloth), and pulled it over his head and around his body, securing it between his legs to make a cloak. He danced, holding his spear high over his head, and the people sang: "*Lubaale nannyini jjoba waliwo ensonga*" (Dear lubaale, the owner of our heads, we have a reason). He then moved to the fire and mixed the ashes and coals with his bare hands, rubbing them over his face as though he were washing in water, making his face white with ash.

A woman sitting next to George whispered to him that it is Kawumpuli, *katikiro* or prime minister of all of the *empewo*, who had come. When he asked her how she knew, since the balubaale had not yet spoken, she told him that only Kawumpuli works with ash. The drummers also began a song that is reserved only for the princes, Bamweyana and Kawumpuli: "*Abalangira ngo- aliira waggulu nga ntaayi*" (The princes eat from above like birds).

Kawumpuli soon returned from the fireplace to dancing, spear raised high, cloak over his head, white ash defining his round features in the glowing space. He sat down on the ground in front of the area with the spears and stuck his spear into the earthen floor in front of him. People came forward to address him, and he clasped their hands in his, squeezing them tightly as they talked with him. China came forward, and he grasped her hands like this too. The connection felt intense.

He said that her grip lacks strength, *amanyi*, that her hands lack it. She replied that this was what she requested, strength. She was thinking of the strength not to become angry with her children when she is tired, the strength to stay calm even when things are difficult. He heard her asking for power, which she clumsily tried to correct.

Irene, coming to her rescue, introduced China and George to Kawumpuli, explaining that we were the ones who helped to organize the drumming. Kawumpuli asked what it is that we wanted done for us, and George explained that we were only asking him to pave the way for whatever we are doing. Kawumpuli turned back to China and explained to George that there were things that she is working on, but that are not yet implemented. That she needs to serve the *misambwa*. Then she will get everything, the power from Buganda. He continued, saying that she is a Nalongo who wants to rescue her nation from immorality that has led to diseases and mental illnesses. He can see that she is a natural Nalongo, and that she feels sympathy for her community, that she is a mother, a kind mother of her nation. He said that she is educated and that she thought she has traveled to Uganda to continue this education. But this is not the case; she has traveled here because she wants to rescue her own country, and her country is suffering because the *misambwa* are angry with it. He went on, saying that here in Uganda people can easily be healed from mental illnesses, but in her country they aren't. Then he started to name the things that China must look for, and George called for his bag so that he could take a pen and paper to help write them down. Kawumpuli said that China must look for a white hen, beads, and a bark cloth and that she would serve the *misambwa*. She should also bring a white goat for the feast, a white sheep for sacrifice, and a white cock for Mukasa, to be thrown alive in the lake.

After he talked to George and China, Kawumpuli stood and began dancing again. He took his spear out of the ground and balanced it on top of his head. As we stood near the edge of the ssabo, Irene came over and introduced us to the man who had been seated next to us. He was Peter, another of those who had been drinking but who Jjajja Kasumba had helped to stop. He was leaving, and George prepared to leave with him too.

Things were quieting down for everyone now. The drummers stopped drumming; everyone was themselves. Things were back to normal. While the light hadn't changed, it was as though the lights had come back on at the end of a performance in a theater. The spell we had all been under was over, and we were in a different frame. Jjajja Kasumba came over to thank us for helping to sponsor the feast, and we thanked him for welcoming us into this beautiful event.

Peter and George started up the road, walking a bit ahead, and they exchanged contacts and made a plan to meet and talk the next day. Peter was home for a month from his work in Rwanda, and we wanted to try to see him before he returned. He got into the Toyota Premio that was parked at the top of the hill. We had seen the car there before, and China had joked that it must be a big night at the ssabo, not realizing who the car belonged to. We got into our car with Noah and drove away, too.

CALL AND RESPONSE

When they are fed and cradled in the laps of the balubaale, roughly bounced and soothed like babies, the basamize at the *ekijjulo* are reminded of their dependency on the *jjajjas*, on the balubaale, on all that has come before them. While the balubaale might not be ancestors in the sense of a traceable line of human descent, the *ekijjulo* and other rituals remind the basamize of their kinship with spirits who have long-standing relationships with their clans and families. Through gestures of care and enforced dependency, the basamize are reminded, in a deeply embodied way, that they are as dependent as infants on these intangible persons. To be clear, in saying this, we are not speaking of the basamize as symbolically becoming infants in these spaces, in the sense of their awaiting a rebirth into a new stage of life, as we might think of it if we were talking about moments of liminality in rites of passage (Turner 1967). Rather, they engage the balubaale—who manifest themselves in the bodies of their companions—with their own bodies as if they were infants or small children engaging with a grandparent, without an eye toward transforming this relationship into something else. In referring to themselves as grandchildren and to the balubaale as grandparents, in feeding and being fed by them, they acknowledge an ethical relationship of dependency and reciprocal care with those spirits, ancestors, and elders who have always and already had a hold on their life.

These enactments of infancy and care speak to the nature of the interruptions that define the experience of recovery for basamize seeking to leave histories of problem drinking behind. Dreams and other signs interrupted the lives of Semuju, Irene, and Amos and called them to tend to the obligations and responsibilities that precede their own existence. These experiences stopped them in their tracks and made them question their lives—and the actions and identities of the more-than-human others who they came to think might have a hold on them. Drawing on the work of Rasmus Dyring (2022) and Lisa Gunther's (2006) readings of Emmanuel Levinas and Gertrude Stein, we want to suggest that these interruptions are "anarchic" in the sense that they call people to return their attention to obligations and responsibilities that were always and already prior to their existence. As Lisa Gunther writes, "anarchy refers to a time before the origin [an-arche], in which I find myself already responsible for the Other before having willingly undertaken to commit myself to such a responsibility. The anarchic response to the Other antecedes and interrupts the projects through which I define myself" (2006, 4–5). In emphasizing this dynamic of responsiveness in these stories we shift the emphasis away from a focus on how people come to determine the meaning of their experiences or how they determine what rules might apply in a given situation, instead looking towards "the point where something challenges [them] and puts [their] own possibilities in question" (Waldenfels 2011, 30).

These questions of responsivity and interruption return us to the questions that lie at the center of our larger project, helping us to construct a model of ethical self-formation and recovery that can more adequately attend to the effects of spiritual experiences in people's processes of ethical transformation. In taking up a focus on anarchic responsivity and interruption, we move beyond approaches that would foreground the human practices that might generate such experiences and refuse ontological questions that would seek to define what the lubaale really are. Like Dyring and Grøn (2021) we instead ask how these anarchic interruptions impact the world that we share. Taking such an approach allows us to attend to the effects of more-than-human beings, God, or other special beings in people's lives, without either requiring us to explain their manifestation as the product of human action or requiring us to make ontological assertions or denials about that which lies beyond us.

EXTROSPECTIVE QUESTIONS

For all of their differences, the people who attend Pastor John's church and the people who visit Jjajja Kasumba's shrine are all working to respond to interruptions of this kind. In their efforts to understand and respond to these interruptions, they all found themselves asking questions about the intangible persons who might be shaping their lives. As in Susan Reynolds Whyte's writings on the ways people confront misfortune in a neighboring area of Eastern Uganda, the questions asked and the answers sought focus less on the introspective question, "Why me?" than they [do] on the extrospective question, "Who are you?" with the "inquiring gaze focused upon beings outside [the self]" (1997, 30). Further, as is also true in Whyte's work, at both the shrine and the church this question is not asked as a matter of abstract curiosity or even regret; instead, it is asked in an effort to determine a course of action, in an effort to respond, to *do* something about the influence of those others who are impinging on one's life. For while a life may be shaped by the actions of spiritual others, there are concrete things that can be done—either to exorcise the spirit, on the one hand, or to repair and more productively attend to the relationship, on the other.

For Semuju, whose story we shared at the opening of this chapter, this process of extrospective questioning led to the revelation that Kiwanuka had sent Bamweyana to punish him for his neglect, to call his attention to the spiritual obligations that were always and already upon him through Kiwanuka's intergenerational ties to his family. Semuju's drinking was neither disease nor moral failing, but rather was a punishment inflicted by a possessing spirit for his neglect of his spiritual duties. By properly attending to Kiwanuka and Bamweyana, Semuju was freed from this punishment while at the same time deepening his ties to Kiwanuka with the hope of prospering through his care.

In learning to see his drinking in this way, Semuju came to understand that there were things he could do to change his situation. Even if we bracket the question of the ontological reality of the balubaale for the moment, we can see that in materially responding to Kiwanuka's call, Semuju's experience of the world was transformed, his sacrifices allowing him to approach the task of living a sober life with a different kind of energy and commitment. Just as a woman might be reoriented toward her struggle with an obstructed birth through the recitation of a therapeutic chant (Levi-Strauss 1963; Jackson 2005; Kirmayer 1993), so was Semuju reoriented toward his struggle with alcohol. Likewise, in coming to understand his relapse and the loss of his job as resulting from the destruction of the kit, the restoration of the kit became the means through which he could reorient himself toward the task of sobriety once again (Scherz, Mpanga, and Namirembe 2022).

While the actions of a spirit like Kiwanuka or Bamweyana might seem to be entirely beyond human control, the ritual restoration of the lubaale kit opened a space of possibility for Semuju. There was something to do that might have an effect, and in this there was a new kind of hope, a new source for renewed strength. Semuju was also both responsible for making the repair and not entirely responsible for its result. Kiwanuka's response to his sacrifice lay beyond his control. While Kiwanuka's positive response to the sacrifice was not owed to Semuju as a guaranteed outcome of a reciprocal exchange (Stroeken 2010), it was a possibility, and in this space of possibility, this opening, lay a hope that life could be different.

While such an understanding of the possible effects of ritual might lead to deadly results in the case of an appendicitis if prayer and ritual were not also accompanied by surgery, we want to argue that, in the case of addiction, such an understanding opens up radically new pathways for reengaging one's future. As we can see in Semuju's story, and in the stories presented in the previous chapter, this process of repositioning oneself in relation to illness is not an easy one, and it may take months or even years to accomplish. But once embraced and symbolically engaged, through ritual speech and action, these understandings of illness can have remarkable effects.

HIGHER POWERS

This process of extrospective questioning and ritual engagement differs from the way the "Higher Power" is engaged in inpatient treatment programs and AA groups. While one may submit to any higher power, the Higher Power in AA—the use of the singular is important here—is envisioned as a benevolent force whose role is primarily to strengthen the will of the alcoholic who has become "powerless over alcohol" so that he can live a sober life, despite his unchangeable condition of being an alcoholic (Antze 1987; Valverde 1998; Brandes 2002). While these images of a singular will-strengthening force and the unchangeable nature of addiction are no doubt present in Uganda, in this book we have shown that they, as a pair, are only one small part of the many ways addictions and higher powers are imagined and engaged.

Ugandan Pentecostals and basamize attempting to overcome alcohol-related problems are less focused on asking God to help strengthen their wills than they are on using rituals to engage directly with the spiritual beings who are affecting their lives. In the stories of people involved in either spiritual warfare or kusamira, we find a model of personhood and agency in which people's actions are influenced by forces that are conceptualized as external and direct. Even more importantly, these influences are also thought to be changeable through prayer and other ritual work, and this opens up a range of possible futures that can be foreclosed in other models. In short, it is less about making oneself strong enough to overcome a permanently determined state, than it is about attempting to deal with the determining spiritual forces directly through ritual means. While this vision of bodies taken over by external forces bears some similarity to the metaphor of the hijacked brain found in discussions of the chronic relapsing brain disease model, at both Pastor John's church and Jjajja Kasumba's ssabo there is something one can do to expel or negotiate with the hijacker. While Pastor John and Jjajja Kasumba are by no means always successful in their efforts, the paths to recovery traversed by Daniella, Richard, Semuju, Amos, and Irene allow us to see potentials contained within other modes of living in relation to addiction by allowing us to see how addictions, and their afters, unfold in a world that has not yet been completely colonized by the chronic disease model.

Conclusion

THE PARTY

The day after the party, our phones started ringing. People were not happy. The assistant pastor at Pastor John's church said that the members of his church who had attended the function claimed we were advocating for the basamize. Jjajja Kasumba felt that he had been attacked by the Pentecostals. "But, of course, we're used to things like that," he added wryly.

Truthfully, we had all been a bit nervous about the party. The clouds were predicting heavy rain, and we were making an attempt to gather people who might not get along. Though they had all struggled with problems with alcohol, they had very different ideas about what should be done to solve them. Nevertheless, we wanted to show our appreciation for the tremendous amount of time people had given us and to recognize those who wanted to be recognized for their contribution to our project. In Uganda, where the social aesthetics of well-being and recognition so often turn on moments of public display (Zoanni 2019), the situation called for a function. And so, we applied for a small grant from the Equity Center at the University of Virginia and, at the end of China's last visit in 2019, we rented a beautiful pavilion on the shore of Lake Victoria. We invited everyone who had contributed to the project in a significant way for a buffet lunch and asked a few whether they would like to share their stories with the assembled group.

Delayed by torrential downpours and muddy roads, people arrived slowly. While they were civil enough with one another, things were clearly tense, especially for the Pentecostals. They were happy to have been invited and looked forward to the opportunity to testify, but also feared that their attendance might expose them to spiritual danger. One refused to eat. Another walked over to the lake to spend some time in prayer. A third expressed his concerns about the writing of a book that would include both his story and the stories of people who had visited basamize.

But even with the palpable tensions, most listened as people came up to the microphone to share their experiences. George, who also works as a professional master of ceremonies for other major functions, handled the job of leading the discussion with great care. Kato, who had stopped drinking after being violently possessed by his mother's ghost (Scherz and Mpanga 2019), encouraged those who were worried to calm down, saying that although he was a Catholic, our book would be a "book of wonders" and that it should include everything, even the stories of the basamize. At the end of the afternoon, one of the waiters who had been serving the lunch requested a chance to speak and came up to the microphone to appreciate those who had spoken and to share his own story of recovery.

In the arguments that played out at the function and in the tense calls that followed over the coming days, the people you have read about on the preceding pages of this book were, at least partly, trying to figure out whether and how it could be possible for a book to include stories told from all these different perspectives. Since personal narratives of the kind being told on the stage that afternoon typically circulate in spiritual tracts—a form of writing that arguably constitutes the most common literary genre in Uganda—it is largely taken for granted that to include a story in a nonfiction book is, at least to some degree, an endorsement of it and its ontological underpinnings. How could we, then, be trying to write a book that was endorsing both spiritual warfare and kusamira, God and the lubaale? Beyond the more complex ontological question of the spiritual problems that might arise from the publication of such a book, wouldn't the book's chapters contradict one another?

TAKING THINGS SERIOUSLY

The people who attended the party were not alone in these concerns. In recent years, anthropologists have hotly debated the question of how we ought to treat the claims others make about the nature of the world, particularly where these claims differ radically from those held by the anthropologists. Even among scholars who may not be deeply invested in the debates of the ontological turn, the injunction to "take seriously" the claims that others make about the very nature of the world has begun to catch on as a political move, as a way of decolonizing academic practice. Embedded within this call is a claim that earlier scholars were not taking the statements that people made quite seriously enough and that, in this failure, anthropologists were neglecting to consider the ways in which their concepts and politics might be transformed by a more serious engagement with the ontological claims of others (Candea 2011; Holbraad and Pedersen 2017; Archambault 2016; De La Cadena 2010; Holbraad and Viveriros de Castro 2016). While the distinction between talking about how cosmology informs a given person's interpretation of their experience and talking about ontology may seem abstract, it is in fact a deeply political distinction. Such ontological questions are no doubt foundational to the "highly politicized and intimate battle over who and what has the right to exist" (Langwick 2010, 232). With such thoughts in mind, anthropologists have been trying to think more carefully about the sorts of violations we commit when we exclude various more-than-human beings from the stories we tell and to find ways to bring them back into our texts (Fernando 2017; Mittermaier 2011; Moll 2018; Watts 2013; Povinelli 2015; Todd 2016; Ramberg 2014; Bawaka Country et al. 2016).

When we began talking with people like Semuju and Daniella, we hoped that we would be able to find an approach that could engage with the ontological presence of these intangible persons in their lives and also hoped that these writings might offer a new path forward that would allow us to avoid explaining away their experiences and these beings. Yet, attending to the agency of such beings across a range of sites where people were deeply invested in asserting their ontological commitments over and against the others that we were also exploring proved to be more complicated than we had originally anticipated. To take one person "seriously" seemed to involve contradicting the views of another. Was Kiwanuka a lubaale spirit who merited our care and reverence, a demon to be exorcised, or nothing at all? Further, we found it increasingly impossible to find a way to live in all of these different "worlds" at the same time.

With these tensions pushed to the foreground, we found ourselves oscillating between a desire to "take seriously" the claims people make about the effects of various copresences in their lives by focusing on the agency of these beings and a less radical approach that would focus on the effects of people's embodied experiences and their interpretations of them. Should we describe the effectiveness of ritual in ways that ignore the possible actions of the divinities and other spirits to whom such rituals might be addressed? Or should we describe those rituals in ways that might include intangible persons as actors whose effects are more than socially or phenomenologically real? Our views on the affordances between these two stances have been shaped by the fact that we are working with people who are both united and fiercely opposed on ontological grounds. While the Pentecostals and basamize who squared off with one another at the party share a permeable or relational model of personhood and subjectivity and an understanding that intangible persons act as powerful causal agents in the world, they stridently disagree with one another about the nature of those beings, about their moral valence, and about the right course of action to take to resolve the problems that they have caused. Working with both groups of people within the same project has shaped the way we think about matters of ontology and has made us more sympathetic to approaches to anthropology that have been cast as insufficiently attentive to the reality of other ways of being in the world.

To be sure, there remains an important gap between arguments that truly unsettle secular ontologies and those that speak only to the affordances and effects of cosmology, interpretation, and experience. Talking about Daniella's sobriety as an effect of her interpretation of her experience of feeling a heaviness moving up and out of her and talking about her sobriety as an effect of her having been successfully delivered from a demon are two very different things. Likewise, to talk of Semuju's sobriety as an effect of his engagement with Kiwanuka as a socially real being through the costly assembly of offerings is quite different from talking about his sobriety, and his relapse, as an effect of Kiwanuka's own actions. Yet, while wanting to maintain a sense of these differences, we have ultimately found the gap between these approaches to be difficult, and perhaps even impossible, to bridge without making commitments to one world over and against others.

This is not to say that the push to think with the term ontology does not do real work. It does. It lets the interpretations of our interlocutors breathe and forces all of us to listen to interpretations that we might otherwise have real reasons to want to explain away.[1] And yet, while ontology is good to think with, it pushes us into one of two problematic alternatives when pushed to its logical conclusions. Either we embrace the ontology of our interlocutors, but become unable to attend to the forms of difference excluded by it, or we craft a more inclusive ontology (such as in Bialecki 2017), but accept that it will most likely be foreign to those we study and may also entail certain logical contradictions (Heywood 2012).

Faced with such possibilities, we have found a return to an older, less radical form of anthropology, or at least an embrace of a certain degree of ambiguity, to be the only viable solution in this case. To be clear, we have indeed endeavored to take seriously our friends' experiences and their interpretations of them. We have not attempted to explain them away, but nevertheless, in the end we have posited some combination of experience, interpretation, and the relations between humans as the causal agents, not God or Kiwanuka. Because of this, the interpretations we have offered lie a long way from our interlocutors' own interpretations. In this, there is an unavoidable gap between this book and what Daniella or Semuju would write if this were their book, or what we would write if we were collaborating with them in a way that would embrace their claims about the world and all the exclusions that those claims might entail.

NOTES

INTRODUCTION

1. To protect the confidentiality of those who participated in the study, with the exception of public figures and readily identifiable public institutions all names and placenames are pseudonyms.

2. For an insightful discussion of the consequences of ignoring the question of alcohol brewing and distillation in the context of wood fuel conservation programs, see (McCall 2002).

3. By 2014, the per capita consumption rate was reduced to 9.8 liters (World Health Organization 2014). An official at the Ugandan Ministry of Health suspected that the drop in the WHO estimated per capita consumption rate was not the result of a change in consumption practices, but a correction following the former inclusion of a lightly fermented porridge, *obushera*, in the earlier count.

4. The Luganda language relies on noun classes to denote different categories. In this book we regularly use the prefixes *Ba-, Mu-, Bu-, Lu-,* and *Ki-* to modify the root *-ganda*. You will see the words *Baganda* (people belonging to the Baganda ethnic group, plural); *Muganda* (a single person belonging to the Baganda ethnic group); *Luganda* (the language the Baganda speak); *Buganda* (the place/kingdom associated with the Baganda); and *Kiganda* (things and ideas of the Baganda).

5. These forms of care were occasionally mentioned in passing in the small body of literature on the treatment of alcohol use disorders in Uganda, but the mentions of these other forms of treatment are invariably brief and almost always made in the context of saying that little is known about these other approaches (Kalema and Vanderplasschen 2015; Kalema et al. 2017; Vorhölter 2017).

6. The average monthly household income in Kampala is approximately 300 USD and 100 USD for the country. The exchange rate during our research was approximately 3600 UGX to 1 USD.

7. While it is impossible to meaningfully include all Kampala's rich ethnic and cultural traditions, it would be a greater mistake to ignore them entirely or to engage with them in an ad hoc or superficial fashion. With this in mind, we chose to limit ourselves to the most common form of indigenous healing found in the greater Kampala area. This is drawn from practices of the Kiganda ethnic group, but people from other ethnic groups also visit these healers.

8. For related reviews of the contemporary state of the medical anthropology of sub-Saharan Africa, see (Mkhwanazi 2016; Obrist and Van Euwijk 2020).

9. For a related analysis of similar trends in the history of medicine in sub-Saharan Africa, see (Schumaker 2001).

10. China wishes to thank historian Marissa Mika for reminding her of this sobering fact.

11. For a comprehensive overview of the anthropology of global mental health, see (Lovell, Read, and Lang 2019).

12. For work on the social determinants of substance abuse, see (Heath 1987; Hunt and Barker 2001; M. Marshall, Ames, and Bennett 2001; Nichter and Quintero 2004; Gamburd 2008; Carr 2010; Knight 2015; Garcia 2010; Schonberg and Bourgois 2009; Bourgois 1995).

1. *BATUZAALA MU BAALA*: SEEKING CONNECTION AND FLOW IN KAMPALA'S BARS

1. While this song is about alcohol, Kartel is himself a Muslim and does not drink.

2. For a detailed account of the impact of colonialism on alcohol production and consumption in Zambia, see (Colson and Scudder 1988).

3. For a more detailed history of the National Alcohol Control Policy of 2019, see (Kalema 2019).

4. For a discussion of the racial politics of a Guinness ad campaign in Ghana and Nigeria, see (J. Roberts 2010).

5. For a discussion of public anxieties over such "detoothing" in Uganda, see (Moore 2020).

6. This phrase is not to be confused with *kulya ssente*, a phrase that can be translated "to eat money" and that generally refers to corruption.

7. Like the university women discussed above, customers who receive drinks bought in this way might eventually return some of them to the bar attendant in exchange for cash, often giving the attendant a cut in exchange for this favor.

2. ONCE AN ADDICT . . . : LEARNING THE CHRONIC RELAPSING BRAIN DISEASE MODEL IN KAMPALA'S REHABILITATION CENTERS

1. With the consent of Dr. David Basangwa, we have not used pseudonyms for Butabika Hospital or for Dr. Basangwa himself.

2. By 2019, a sizable new dormitory had been constructed just behind the first.

3. For a quantitative study of Alcohol Use Disorder treatment outcomes at Butabika Hospital, see (Kalani 2019).

4. For a discussion of the theme of potential in relation to empowerment programming in Uganda, see (Moore 2016).

5. The idea that addiction might be a more or less permanent condition drew on an earlier body of work carried out with primates and prisoners during the mid-twentieth century at the monkey colony at the University of Michigan at Ann Arbor, and at the Addiction Research Center, a basic science laboratory that was once part of a federal prison-hospital in Lexington, Kentucky. These scientists hoped to continue the work of the turn-of-the century clinicians who sought to define addiction as a disease and to move it from the moral domain of the will into the medical domain of the body (Campbell 2007). The midcentury research carried out at Ann Arbor and Lexington differed from the earlier work in several important ways. Clinicians working at the turn of the twentieth century were trying to find a cure for addiction. Working in relative isolation, they proposed a mindbogglingly diverse range of techniques and corresponding theories of the physiological causes of addiction. By midcentury, the Ann Arbor and Lexington researchers were unified under a national coordinating committee and were consequently more focused on developing a single cohesive model of addiction. These researchers also differed from their predecessors in their growing sense that addiction might, in some cases, be incurable.

3. PUT SOMETHING IN HIS DRINK: SENSORY SHIFTS IN KAMPALA'S HERBAL MEDICINE SHOPS

1. For a more extensive discussion of this point, see (Scherz and Mpanga 2019). For comparative cases related to violence and addiction treatment in Mexico City and Guatemala City, see (Garcia 2015) and (O'Neill 2019).

2. Stacey Langwick's (2010) discussion of the history of the categories of traditional medicine and witchcraft in Tanzania provides an instructive point of comparison. Langwick notes that prior to the 1928 Witchcraft Ordinance in Tanzania, two forms of practice, both concerned with the use of material and mystical means, were recognized. The first set of practices, captured by the term *uganga*, concerned the beneficent use of these various means as they were put towards the aim of healing, while a second term, *uchawi*, was used to indicate the use of material and mystical means for the purposes of harming others. While these sets of practices, and the practitioners who deployed them, were previously held to be quite separate, the 1928 Witchcraft Ordinance combined all acts of "sorcery, enchantment, bewitching, or the purported exercise of any occult power, or the purported possession of any occult knowledge" (48) under the sign of witchcraft, whether or not that knowledge was being used with the intent of helping or harming. At the same time, there was a codification of forms of "native medicine" that could be extracted from their mystical associations and subjected to the scientific discipline of clinical trials and laboratory testing. These trials, which were not unlike those of interest to Dr. Akello, became an increasingly important goal for the colonial government of Tanzania. In looking to Tanzania for inspiration, the NRM government saw the possibility of separating a form of traditional medicine that could be regulated and subjected to scientific testing from the forms of "witchcraft" they saw as both dangerous and distracting.

3. With these concerns in mind, we will not be naming any of the plants used by the herbalists who graciously agreed to allow us to speak with their patients and invited us into their shops and clinics. While the herbalists we spoke with shared many plant names with us, they did so on the condition that we would not share the names of those plants in our writings. Their refusals were less about the history of ethnography and its relation to

colonial power (Simpson 2014), and more about their concerns regarding contemporary bioprospecting (Osseo-Asare 2014; Hayden 2003) and the possibility of being left out of whatever lucrative deals might result from this knowledge.

4. For a discussion of the ontological politics that shape conflicts between, on the one hand, Ghanian scientists focused on synergistic approaches to plant medicines that take into account the possible interactions between different chemicals naturally present in a single plant, and on the other, the focus on extracting individual compounds favored by their Japanese collaborators, see (Droney 2017).

5. The possibility of innate participation in the occult is limited perhaps to occasional stories about *abasezi*, night dancers, who are reported to eat human flesh from fresh graves (cf. Beattie 1963).

6. Disulfiram and disulfiram placebos have largely replaced apomorphine treatment in Russia since the 1980s. Also known as Antabuse and Esperal, disulfiram affects the body's ability to metabolize ethanol. When a person taking disulfiram drinks, high levels of the toxic byproduct acetaldehyde build up in their body and this results in extremely unpleasant flushing, nausea, and high blood pressure. Disulfiram remains commonly used as treatment for alcohol addiction in Denmark and more rarely in the United States (Raikhel 2016).

7. The standard approach to bioethics used in the United States relies on the balancing of four principles—autonomy, beneficence, nonmaleficence, and justice (Beauchamp and Childress 1979). Administering any form of treatment, let alone an aversion therapy, without a patient's knowledge and consent would be seen as running afoul of the principle of autonomy.

4. NOT YOU: HOPING FOR DELIVERANCE IN KAMPALA'S PENTECOSTAL CHURCHES

1. For discussions of the history of spiritual warfare, see (R. Marshall 2016; McCloud 2015) For a history of the ways in which similar practices and models of atonement emerged in Ghana around figures of the pre-Christian Ewe cosmology through the interactions between German Pietist missionaries and early Ewe converts, see (Meyer 1999). For further explorations of the relationship between Pentecostalism and witchcraft discourses in Africa and Melanesia, see (Knut, MacCarthy, and Blanes 2017).

2. For additional reading on the relationship between the embrace of Protestantism and shifts in drinking practices, see (Brusco 1995; Eber 2000; Brandes 2002).

3. On the importance of narrative hope for recovery, see (Bartlett 2020). On hope and Pentecostalism in Zimbabwe see (Maxwell 2005).

4. For a contrasting account of Pentecostal dreaming, see (Eves 2011).

5. CALL AND RESPONSE: RESPONDING TO SPIRITS IN KAMPALA'S SHRINES

1. While we are concerned with the role that spirit possession plays in situations of healing and suffering, we are not seeking to develop a universalizing medicalized account of spirit possession (cf. Ward 1980). Instead, our work is inspired by the writings of scholars who have sought to describe the place of these practices, beliefs, and forms of attachment on their own terms (Boddy 1989; Janzen 1992; Thornton 2017; Lambek 1981;

Stoller 1989; Masquelier 2001; Leistle 2014; van de Port 2011; Beliso-De Jesus 2015; Victor 2019; Crapanzano 1980; Sharp 1994; Crapanzano and Garrison 1977; Igreja, Dias-Lambranca, and Richters 2008). For reviews of this vast and wide ranging literature, see (Boddy 1994; Igreja 2018).

2. These rituals can be linked to a broader constellation of practices related to mediumship that emerged in the Great Lakes region sometime between the thirteenth and sixteenth centuries (Berger 1973; Doyle 2007; Kodesh 2010; Schoenbrun 1998; Beattie 1969) and which today stretches in various forms from Western Uganda to Western Tanzania. While most of the academic writings on these practices are historical, a few anthropologists and ethnomusicologists have worked among contemporary practitioners of kusamira (Hoesing 2012, 2021) and other related traditions (Stroeken 2010).

3. For an insightful discussion of the role of dreaming in colonial politics in Uganda, see (Earle 2017).

4. Tanda is a sacred site in Mityana District. The deep pits scattered across the forest are said to be those dug by the brothers Kayikuzi and Walumbe. For more on the story of Kintu, Nambi, Kayikuzi, and Walumbe, see (Kizza 2010).

5. The basamize we met during the course of this study who also practice Christianity or Islam tend to be open about their other religious commitments in the space of the shrine. They might, for example, wear a rosary around their neck or refuse the food offered at a feast when they are fasting for Ramadan. That said, their participation in kusamira might not be obvious to others in their Christian and Muslim communities as they conduct their engagements with indigenous religious practitioners with greater and lesser degrees of secrecy. It also seems important to say that many, if not most, Christians and Muslims in Uganda openly denounce the practices of the basamize. Jjajja Kasumba often equates lubaale with Christian angels and is emphatic about the fact that Katonda is the one God for all, but this same position would not be taken by many Christians and Muslims in Uganda.

6. For an insightful discussion of gender and the place of baakisimba dance and drumming in Kiganda society outside of the context of kusamira rituals, see (Nannyonga-Tamusuza 2005).

CONCLUSION

1. China wishes to thank Mayanthi Fernando for a generative conversation on this point.

Adu-gyamfi, Samuel, and Eugenia Ama Anderson. 2019. "Indigenous Medicine and Traditional Healing in Africa: A Systematic Synthesis of the Literature." *Philosophy, Social and Human Disciplines* 1: 69–100.

Ahimbisibwe, Patience. 2010. "Coping with Blindness after Drinking Adulterated Waragi." *The Monitor*, October 2, 2010, sec. National. http://www.monitor.co.ug/News/National/-/688334/1022096/-/cn3geyz/-/index.html.

Akyeampong, Emmanuel. 1997. *Drink, Power, and Cultural Change: A Social History of Alcohol in Ghana, c. 1800 to Recent Times*. London: Heinemann.

Anguyo, Innocent, and Simon Masaba. 2012. "Local Gin Claims 4, Blinds 3 in Kampala." *The New Vision*, 2012, December 5 edition, sec. National.

Antze, Paul. 1987. "Symbolic Action in Alcoholics Anonymous." In *Constructive Drinking: Perspectives on Drink from Anthropology*, 149–81. London: Routledge.

Archambault, Julie Soleil. 2016. "Taking Love Seriously in Human-Plant Relations in Mozambique: Toward an Anthropology of Affective Encounters." *Cultural Anthropology* 31 (2): 244–71.

Aulén, Gustav. 2010. *Christus Victor: An Historical Study of the Three Main Types of the Idea of the Atonement*. Translated by A. G. Hebert. London: Society for Promoting Christian Knowledge.

Bajunirwe, Francis, David R. Bangsberg, and Ajay K. Sethi. 2013. "Alcohol Use and HIV Serostatus of Partner Predict High-Risk Sexual Behavior among Patients Receiving Antiretroviral Therapy in South Western Uganda." *BMC Public Health* 13 (1): 1–7.

Bakke, Øystein, and Dag Endal. 2010. "Vested Interests in Addiction Research and Policy Alcohol Policies Out of Context: Drinks Industry Supplanting Government Role in Alcohol Policies in Sub-Saharan Africa." *Addiction* 105 (1): 22–28.

Bartlett, Nicholas. 2020. *Recovering Histories: Life and Labor After Heroin in Reform-Era China*. Berkeley: University of California Press.

Bartlett, Nicholas, William Garriott, and Eugene Raikhel. 2014. "What's in the 'Treatment Gap'? Ethnographic Perspectives on Addiction and Global Mental Health from China, Russia, and the United States." *Medical Anthropology* 33 (6): 457–77.

Bawaka Country, S. Wright, S. Suchet-Pearson, K. Lloyd, L. Burarrwanga, R. Ganambarr, and D. Maymuru. 2016. "The Politics of Ontology and Ontological Politics." *Dialogues in Humana Geography* 6 (1): 23–27.

Beaglehole, Robert, and Ruth Bonita. 2009. "Alcohol: A Global Priority." *The Lancet* 373 (9682): 2173–74.

Beattie, John. 1963. "Sorcery in Bunyoro." In *Witchcraft and Sorcery in East Africa*, edited by John Middleton and Edward H. Winter, 27–55. London: Routledge and Kegan Paul.

———. 1969. "Spirit Mediumship in Bunyoro." In *Spirit Mediumship and Society in Africa*, edited by John Beattie and J. Middleton, 159–170. New York: Routledge and Kegan Paul.

Beauchamp, Tom, and James Childress. 1979. *Principles of Biomedical Ethics*. New York: Oxford University Press.

Bejarano, Carolina Alonso, Lucia Lopez Juarez, Mirian A. Mijangos Garcia, and Daniel Goldstein. 2019. *Decolonizing Ethnography: Undocumented Immigrants and New Directions in Social Science*. Durham, NC: Duke University Press.

Beliso-De Jesus, Aisha M. 2015. *Electric Santeria: Racial and Sexual Assemblages of Transnational Religion*. New York: Columbia University Press.

Benton, Adia. 2015. *HIV Exceptionalism: Development Through Disease in Sierra Leone*. Minneapolis: University of Minnesota Press.

Berger, Iris. 1973. *The Kubandwa Religious Complex of Interlacustrine East Africa: A Historical Study, c. 1500–1900*. Madison: University of Wisconsin-Madison.

Bialecki, Jon. 2017. *A Diagram for Fire: Miracles and Variation in an American Charismatic Movement*. Berkeley: University of California Press.

Bialecki, Jon, and Girish Daswani. 2015. "Introduction: What Is an Individual? The View from Christianity." *HAU: Journal of Ethnographic Theory* 5 (1).

p'Bitek, Okot. 1971. *African Religions in Western Scholarship*. Nairobi: East African Literature Bureau.

Boddy, Janice. 1989. *Wombs and Alien Spirits: Women, Men, and the Zar Cult in Northern Sudan*. Madison: University of Wisconsin Press.

———. 1994. "Spirit Possession Revisited: Beyond Instrumentality." *Annual Review of Anthropology* 23: 407–34.

Borovoy, Amy. 2005. *The Too-Good Wife: Alcohol, Codependency, and the Politics of Nurturance in Postwar Japan*. Berkeley: University of California Press.

Bourdieu, Pierre. 1984. *Distinction: A Social Critique of the Judgement of Taste*. New York: Routledge.

Bourgois, Philippe. 1995. *In Search of Respect: Selling Crack in El Barrio*. Cambridge: Cambridge University Press.

Boyd, Lydia. 2015. *Preaching Prevention: Born-Again Christianity and the Moral Politics of AIDS in Uganda*. Athens: Ohio University Press.

Brandes, Stanley. 2002. *Staying Sober in Mexico City*. Austin: University of Texas Press.

Brett, E. A. 1972. *Colonialism and Underdevelopment in East Africa*. Oxford: Oxford University Press.

Brodwin, Paul. 2013. *Everyday Ethics Voices from the Front Line of Community Psychiatry*. Berkeley: University of California Press.

Brusco, Elizabeth. 1995. *The Reformation of Machismo. Evangelical Conversion and Gender in Colombia*. Austin: University of Texas Press.

Bubandt, Nils. 2014. *The Empty Seashell: Witchcraft and Doubt on an Indonesian Island*. Ithaca: Cornell University Press.

Campbell, Nancy. 2007. *Discovering Addiction: The Science and Politics of Substance Abuse Research*. Ann Arbor: University Michigan Press.

Campbell, Nancy D. 2010. "Toward a Critical Neuroscience of 'Addiction.'" BioSocieties 5 (1): 89–104.

Candea, Matei. 2011. "Endo/Exo." Common Knowledge 17 (1): 146–150.

Carr, Summerson. 2010. *Scripting Addiction: The Politics of Therapeutic Talk and American Sobriety*. Princeton, NJ: Princeton University Press.

Cassaniti, Julia, and Tanya Luhrmann. 2014. "The Cultural Kindling of Spiritual Experience." *Current Anthropology* 55 (10): 333–43.

Chakrabarty, Dipesh. 1997. "The Time of History and the Times of Gods." In *The Politics of Culture in the Shadow of Capital*, edited by Lisa Lowe and David Lloyd. Durham: Duke University Press.

Cole, Jennifer, and Lynn Thomas. 2009. *Love in Africa*: Chicago: University of Chicago Press.

Coleman, Simon. 2011. "Introduction: Negotiating Personhood in African Christianities." *Journal of Religion in Africa* 41 (3): 243–55.

Colson, Elizabeth, and Thayer Scudder. 1988. *For Prayer and Profit : The Ritual, Economic, and Social Importance of Beer in Gwembe District, Zambia, 1950–1982*. Stanford: Stanford University Press.

Comaroff, Jean. 1981. "Healing and Cultural Transformation: The Tswana of Southern Africa." *Social Science and Medicine* 15B: 367–78.

Comaroff, Jean, and John Comaroff. 2001. "On Personhood: An Anthropological Perspective from Africa." *Social Identities* 7 (2): 267–83.

Cook, P. 1971. "Cancer of the Oesophagus in Africa. A Summary and Evaluation of the Evidence for the Frequency of Occurrence, and a Preliminary Indication of the Possible Association with the Consumption of Alcoholic Drinks Made from Maize." *British Journal of Cancer* 25 (4): 853–80.

Courtwright, David T. 2010. "The NIDA Brain Disease Paradigm: History, Resistance and Spinoffs." *BioSocieties* 5 (1): 137–47.

Covington-Ward, Yolanda. 2016. *Gesture and Power: Religion, Nationalism, and Everyday Performance in Congo*. Durham, NC: Duke University Press.

Crapanzano, Vincent. 1980. *Tuhami: Portrait of a Moroccan*. Chicago: University of Chicago Press.

Crapanzano, Vincent, and Vivian Garrison. 1977. *Case Studies in Spirit Possession*. New York: John Wiley.

Crush, Jonathan, and Charles Ambler, eds. 1992. *Liquor and Labor in Southern Africa*. Athens: Ohio University Press.

Csordas, Thomas. 2002. *Body, Meaning, Healing*. New York: Springer.

———. 1997. *The Sacred Self: A Cultural Phenomenology of Charismatic Healing*. Berkeley: University of California Press.

Culbreth, Rachel, Katherine Masyn, Monica H. Swahn, Shannon Self-Brown, and Rogers Kasirye. 2021. "The Interrelationships of Child Maltreatment, Alcohol Use, and Suicidal

Ideation among Youth Living in the Slums of Kampala, Uganda." *Child Abuse & Neglect* 112 (3).

Das, Veena, and Clara Han, eds. 2015. *Living and Dying in the Contemporary World: A Compendium*. Oakland: University of California Press.

Daswani, Girish. 2011. "(In-)Dividual Pentecostals in Ghana." *Journal of Religion in Africa* 41 (3): 256–79.

———. 2015. *Looking Back, Moving Forward: Transformation and Ethical Practice in the Ghanaian Church of Pentecost*. Toronto: University of Toronto Press.

De La Cadena, Marisol. 2010. "Indigenous Cosmopolitics in the Andes: Conceptual Reflections beyond 'Politics.'" *Cultural Anthropology* 25 (2): 334–70.

Deger, Jennifer. 2006. *Shimmering Screens: Making Media in an Aboriginal Community*. Minneapolis: University of Minnesota Press.

Dobler, Gregor. 2010. "License to Drink: Between Liberation and Inebriation in Northern Namibia." In *Beer in Africa: Drinking Spaces, States, and Selves*, edited by Steven van Wolputte and Mattia Fumanti, 167–192. New Brunswick: Transaction Publishers.

Doherty, Jacob. 2021. *Waste Worlds: Inhabiting Kampala's Infrastructures of Disposability*. Oakland: University of California Press.

———. 2017. "Life (and limb) in the fast-lane: disposable people as infrastructure in Kampala's boda boda industry." *Critical African Studies* 9 (2): 192–209.

Douglas, Mary, ed. 1987. *Constructive Drinking: Perspectives on Drink from Anthropology*. Cambridge: Cambridge University Press.

Doyle, Shane. 2007. "The Cwezi-Kubandwa Debate: Gender, Hegemony and Pre-Colonial Religion in Bunyoro, Western Uganda." *Africa* 77 (4): 559–81.

Droney, Damien. 2014. "Ironies of Laboratory Work During Ghana's Second Age of Optimism." *Cultural Anthropology* 29 (2): 363–84.

———. 2017. "Scientific Capacity Building and the Ontologies of Herbal Medicine in Ghana." *Canadian Journal of African Studies* 50 (3): 437–54.

Dyring, Rasmus. 2022. "On the Silent Anarchy of Intimacy Images of Alterity, Openness and Sociality in Life with Dementia." In *Imagistic Care: Growing Old in a Precarious World*, edited by Cheryl Mattingly and Lone Grøn, 109–36. New York: Fordham University Press.

Dyring, Rasmus, and Lone Grøn. 2022. "Ellen and the Little One : A Critical Phenomenology of Potentiality in Life with Dementia." *Anthropological Theory* 22 (1): 3–25.

Earle, Jonathon. 2017. "Dreams and Political Imagination in Colonial Buganda." *The Journal of African History* 58 (1): 85–105.

Eber, Christine. 2010. *Women and Alcohol in a Highland Maya Town: Water of Hope, Water of Sorrow*. Austin: University of Texas Press.

Edyegu, Daniel. 2009. "Alcohol Ruins Nabumali High School." *The New Vision*, June 15, 2009, sec. National. http://www.newvision.co.ug/D/8/13/684867.

Eisenstein, Anna. 2021. "On Waiting Willfully in Urban Uganda: Toward an Anthropology of Pace." *Cultural Anthropology* 36 (3): 458–83.

Elyachar, Julia. 2005. *Markets of Dispossession: NGOs, Economic Development, and the State in Cairo*. Durham: Duke University Press.

Euromonitor Consulting. 2016. "Market Analysis for Illicit Alcohol in Uganda." Kampala: Nile Breweries Limited.

Evans-Pritchard, E. E. 1937. *Witchcraft, Oracles and Magic among the Azande*. Oxford: Clarendon Press.

Eves, Richard. 2011. "Pentecostal Dreaming and Technologies of Governmentality in a Melanesian Society." *American Ethnologist* 38 (4): 758–73.

Fabian, Johannes. 1983. *Time and the Other: How Anthropology Makes Its Object*. New York: Columbia University Press.

Faubion, James D. 2011. *An Anthropology of Ethics*. Cambridge: Cambridge University Press.

Ferguson, James. 2013. "Declarations of Dependence: Labor, Personhood, and Welfare in South Africa." *Journal of the Royal Anthropological Institute* 19: 223–42.

Fernando, Mayanthi. 2017. "Supernatureculture." *The Immanent Frame* (blog). 2017. https://tif.ssrc.org/2017/12/11/supernatureculture.

Foucault, Michel. 1990. *The Use of Pleasure. The History of Sexuality: Volume Two*. New York: Vintage Books.

———. 1997. "Polemics, Politics, and Problematizations: An Interview with Michel Foucault." In *Ethics, Subjectivity and Truth. Essential Works of Michel Foucault*, edited by Paul Rabinow, 382–90. New York: The New Press.

———. 2005. *Hermeneutics of the Subject: Lectures at the Collège de France 1981–1982*. New York: Palgrave Macmillian.

———. 2009. *Security, Population, Territory: Lectures at the College de France, 1977–1978*. Translated by Graham Burchell. London: Picador.

Fullwiley, Duana. 2010. "Revaluating Genetic Causation: Biology, Economy, and Kinship in Dakar, Senegal." *American Ethnologist* 37 (4): 638–61.

Gamburd, Michele Ruth. 2008. *Breaking the Ashes: The Culture of Illicit Liquor in Sri Lanka*. Ithaca, NY: Cornell University Press.

Garcia, Angela. 2010. *The Pastoral Clinic: Addiction and Dispossession along the Rio Grande*. Berkeley: University of California Press.

———. 2015. "Serenity: Violence, Inequality, and Recovery on the Edge of Mexico City." *Medical Anthropology Quarterly*, 1–18.

Gatsiounis, Ioannis. 2010. "The Battle to Stop Drink from Destroying Uganda." *Time*, May 19, 2010. http://content.time.com/time/world/article/0,8599,1989842,00.html.

Geissler, Wenzel, and Ruth Jane Prince. 2010. *The Land Is Dying: Contingency, Creativity and Conflict in Western Kenya*. New York: Berghahn Books.

Gibson, Ian. 2017. *Suffering and Hope: Christianity and Ethics among the Newars of Bhaktapur*. Kathmandu: Ekta Books.

Gifford, Paul. 2004. *Ghana's New Christianity: Pentecostalism in a Globalizing African Economy*. Bloomington: Indiana University Press.

Goffman, Erving. 1959. *The Presentation of Self in Everyday Life*. Garden City: Doubleday.

———. 1986. *Stigma: Notes of the Management of a Spoiled Identity*. New York: Simon and Schuster.

Goldstone, Brian. 2017. "A Prayer's Chance: The Scandal of Mental Health in West Africa." *Harper's Magazine*, 2017.

Good, Mary-Jo DelVecchio. 2001. "The Biotechnical Embrace." *Culture, Medicine, and Psychiatry* 25: 395–410.

Greco, Elisa, Giuliano Martiniello, and Jorg Wiegratz, eds. 2018. *Uganda: The Dynamics of Neoliberal Transformation*. London: Zed Books.

Gunther, Lisa. 2006. *The Gift of the Other: Levinas and the Politics of Reproduction*. Albany: SUNY Press.

Guyer, Jane. 1995. "Wealth in People as Wealth in Knowledge: Accumulation and Composition in Equatorial Africa." *Journal of African History* 36: 91–120.

Hacking, Ian. 1986. "Making Up People." In *Reconstructing Individualism*, edited by T. Heller, M. Sosna, and D. Wellbery, 222–36. Stanford, CA: Stanford University Press.

———. 1990. *The Taming of Chance*. Cambridge: Cambridge University Press.

Hamdy, Sherine. 2012. *Our Bodies Belong to God: Organ Transplants, Islam, and the Struggle for Human Dignity in Egypt*. Berkeley: University of California Press.

Hammer, Rachel, Molly Dingel, Jenny Ostergren, Brad Partridge, Jennifer McCormick, and Barbara Koenig. 2013. "Addiction: Current Criticism of the Brain Disease Paradigm." *AJOB Neuroscience* 4 (3): 27–32.

Hannig, Anita. 2017. *Beyond Surgery: Injury, Healing, and Religion at an Ethiopian Hospital*. Chicago: University of Chicago Press.

Hansen, Helena. 2018. *Addicted to Christ: Remaking Men in Puerto Rican Pentecostal Drug Ministries*. Berkeley: University of California Press.

Hanson, Holly Elisabeth. 2003. *Landed Obligation: The Practice of Power in Buganda*. Portsmouth, NH: Heinemann.

———. 2009. "Mapping Conflict: Heterarchy and Accountability in the Ancient Capital of Buganda." *Journal of African History* 50: 179–202.

Harris, Shana. 2016. "The Social Practice of Harm Reduction in Argentina: A 'Latin' Kind of Intervention." *Human Organization* 75 (1): 1–9.

Hayden, Cori. 2003. *When Nature Goes Public: The Making and Unmaking of Bioprospecting in Mexico*. Princeton, NJ: Princeton University Press.

Heap, Simon. 1998. "'We Think Prohibition Is a Farce': Drinking in the Alcohol-Prohibited Zone of Colonial Northern Nigeria." *International Journal of African Historical Studies* 31 (1): 23–51.

Heath, Dwight B. 1987. "Anthropology and Alcohol Studies: Current Issues." *Annual Review of Anthropology* 16: 99–120.

———. 1995. *International Handbook on Alcohol and Culture*. Westport, CT: Greenwood Press.

de Heusch, Luc. 1981. *Why Marry Her? Society and Symbolic Structures*. Translated by Janet Lloyd. Cambridge: Cambridge University Press.

Heywood, Paolo. 2012. "Anthropology and What There Is: Reflections on 'Ontology.'" *The Cambridge Journal of Anthropology* 30 (1): 143–51.

Hoesing, Peter. 2012. "Kusamira: Singing Rituals of Wellness in Southern Uganda." *African Music* 9 (2): 94–127.

———. 2021. *Kusamira Music in Uganda: Spirit Mediumship and Ritual Healing*. Champaign: University of Illinois Press.

Holbraad, Martin, and Morten Axel Pedersen. 2017. *The Ontological Turn: An Anthropological Exposition*. Cambridge: Cambridge University Press.

Holbraad, Martin, and Eduardo Viveiros de Castro. 2016. "Ideas of Savage Reason: Glass Bead in Conversation with Martin Holbraad and Eduardo Viveiros de Castro." *Glass Bead Site 0: Castalia, the Game of Ends and Means*. https://www.glass-bead.org/article/ideas-of-savage-reason-glass-bead-in-conversation-with-martin-holbraad-and-eduardo-viveiros-de-castro.

Howes, David. 2019. "Mulltisensory Anthropology." *Annual Review of Anthropology* 48: 17–28.

Hunt, G., and J. C. Barker. 2001. "Socio-Cultural Anthropology and Alcohol and Drug Research: Towards a Unified Theory." *Social Science & Medicine (1982)* 53 (2): 165–88.

Igreja, Victor. 2018. "Spirit Possession." In *The International Encyclopedia of Anthropology*, 1–9. Oxford: John Wiley & Sons.

Igreja, Victor, Beatrice Dias-Lambranca, and Annemiek Richters. 2008. "Gamba Spirits, Gender Relations, and Healing in Post-Civil War Gorongosa, Mozambique." *Journal of the Royal Anthropological Institute* 14: 350–67.

Illiffe, John. 1998. *East African Doctors: A History of the Modern Profession*. Cambridge: Cambridge University Press.

Ingold, Tim. 2017. "On Human Correspondence." *Journal of the Royal Anthropological Institute* 23 (1): 9–27.

Jackson, Michael. 2005. *Existential Anthropology: Events, Exigencies, and Effects*. New York: Berghahn Books.

Janzen, John. 1982. *The Quest for Therapy in Lower Zaire*. Berkeley: University of California Press.

———. 1992. *Ngoma : Discourses of Healing in Central and Southern Africa*. Berkeley: University of California Press.

Jones, Jeremy. 2010. "'Nothing Is Straight in Zimbabwe': The Rise of the Kukiya-Kiya Economy 2000–2008." *Journal of Southern African Studies* 36 (2): 285–99.

Kabwama, Steven Ndugwa, Sheila Ndyanabangi, Gerald Mutungi, Ronald Wesonga, Silver Bahendeka, and David Guwatudde. 2016. "Alcohol Use Among Adults in Uganda: Findings from the Countrywide Non-Communicable Disease Risk Factor Cross-Sectional Survey." *Global Health Action* 9 (1): 1–8.

Kagaayi, Joseph, Ronald H. Gray, Christopher Whalen, Pingfu Fu, Duncan Neuhauser, Janet W. McGrath, Nelson K. Sewankambo, et al. 2014. "Indices to Measure Risk of HIV Acquisition in Rakai, Uganda." *PLoS ONE* 9 (4): e92015.

Kalani, Kenneth. 2019. "Prevalence of Relapse of Alcohol Use Disorder and the Association with Self-Efficacy and Perceived Social Support in Butabika Hospital." Master's Thesis, Makerere University.

Kalema, David. 2019. "The Long Journey to Alcohol Policy In Uganda." *Movendi International* October 20, 2019. https://movendi.ngo/blog/2019/10/20/the-long-journey-to-alcohol-policy-in-uganda.

Kalema, David, and Wouter Vanderplasschen. 2015. "Features and Challenges of Alcohol Abuse Treatment in Uganda." *African Journal of Drug & Alcohol Studies* 14 (2): 125–35.

Kalema, David, Wouter Vanderplasschen, Sofie Vindevogel, Ilse Derluyn, and Peter Baguma. 2017. "Treatment Challenges for Alcohol Service Users in Kampala, Uganda." *The International Journal of Alcohol and Drug Research* 6 (1): 27–35.

Karamagi, C. A., J. K. Tumwine, T. Tylleskar, and K. Heggenhougen. 2006. "Intimate Partner Violence against Women in Eastern Uganda: Implications for HIV Prevention." *BMC Public Health* 6: 284.

Keane, Webb. 2016. *Ethical Life: Its Natural and Social Histories*. Princeton, NJ: Princeton University Press.

Kemigisha, Gloria. 2009. "I Had to Get My Husband to Love Me Again." *The Monitor*, October 23, 2009, sec. Fashion & Beauty. http://www.monitor.co.ug/LifeStyle/Fashion Beauty/-/691228/722552/-/na06kg/-/index.html.

Kerridge, Bradley T., Delivette Castor, Phu Tran, Matthew Barnhart, and Roger Pickering. 2014. "Association Between Intoxication at Last Sexual Intercourse and Unprotected Sex Among Men and Women in Uganda." *Journal of Infection in Developing Countries* 8 (11): 1461–69.

Kirenga, Bruce J., Willy Ssengooba, Catherine Muwonge, Lydia Nakiyingi, Stephen Kyaligonza, Samuel Kasozi, Frank Mugabe, Martin Boeree, Moses Joloba, and Alphonse Okwera. 2015. "Tuberculosis Risk Factors among Tuberculosis Patients in Kampala, Uganda: Implications for Tuberculosis Control." *BMC Public Health* 15 (1): 498–511.

Kirmayer, Laurence J. 1993. "Healing and the Invention of Metaphor: The Effectiveness of Symbols Revisited." *Culture Medicine and Psychiatry* 17 (2): 161–95.

———. 2004. "The Cultural Diversity of Healing: Meaning, Metaphor and Mechanism." *British Medical Bulletin* 69: 33–48.

Kiwanuka, Noah, Ali Ssetaala, Juliet Mpendo, Matthias Wambuzi, Annet Nanvubya, Simon Sigirenda, Annet Nalutaaya, et al. 2013. "High HIV-1 Prevalence, Risk Behaviours, and Willingness to Participate in HIV Vaccine Trials in Fishing Communities on Lake Victoria, Uganda." *Journal of the International AIDS Society* 16 (1): 1–8.

Kizza, Immaculate N. 2010. *The Oral Tradition of the Baganda of Uganda: A Study and Anthology of Legends, Myths, Epigrams and Folktales*. Jefferson, NC: McFarland.

Klaits, Fred. 2010. *Death in a Church of Life: Moral Passion during Botswana's Time of AIDS*. Berkeley: University of California Press.

Kleinman, Arthur, Leon Eisenberg, and Byron Good. 1978. "Culture, Illness, and Care: Clinical Lessons from Anthropological and Cross-Cultural Research." *Annals of Internal Medicine* 88: 251–88.

Knight, Kelly Ray. 2015. *addicted.pregnant.poor*. Durham, NC: Duke University Press.

Knut, Rio, Michelle MacCarthy, and Ruy Blanes, eds. 2017. *Pentecostalism and Witchcraft: Spiritual Warfare in Africa and Melanesia*. Basingstoke, UK: Palgrave MacMillan.

Kodesh, Neil. 2010. *Beyond the Royal Gaze: Clanship and Public Healing in Buganda*. Charlottesville: University of Virginia Press.

Kohn, Eduardo. 2015. "Anthropology of Ontologies." *Annual Review of Anthropology* 44: 311–27.

Kopytoff, Igor. 1971. "Ancestors as Elders." *Africa* 41 (2): 129–42.

Kopytoff, Igor, and Suzanne Miers, eds. 1977. *Slavery in Africa: Historical and Anthropological Perspectives*. Madison: University of Wisconsin Press.

Kubrick, Stanley, dir. 1971. *A Clockwork Orange*. United States: Warner Bros.

La Hausse, Paul. 1988. *Brewers, Beerhalls, and Boycotts : A History of Liquor in South Africa*. Johannesburg: Ravan Press.

Laidlaw, James. 2002. "For an Anthropology of Ethics and Freedom." *Journal of the Royal Anthropological Institute* 8 (2): 311–32.

———. 2013. *The Subject of Virtue: An Anthropology of Ethics and Freedom*. Cambridge: Cambridge University Press.

Lambek, Michael. 1981. *Human Spirits: A Cultural Account of Trance in Mayotte*. Cambridge: Cambridge University Press.

———. 2010. "How to Make Up One's Mind: Reason, Passion, and Ethics in Spirit Possession." *University of Toronto Quarterly* 79 (2): 720–41.

———. 2015. *The Ethical Condition: Essays on Action, Person, and Value*. Chicago: University of Chicago Press.

Langwick, Stacey. 2008. "Articulate(d) Bodies: Traditional Medicine in a Tanzanian Hospital." *American Ethnologist* 35 (3): 428–39.

———. 2010. *Bodies, Politics, and African Healing: The Matter of Maladies in Tanzania.* Bloomington: Indiana University Press.

———. 2015. "Partial Publics: The Political Promise of Traditional Medicine in Africa." *Current Anthropology* 56 (4): 493–514.

———. 2018. "A Politics of Habitability: Plants, Healing, and Sovereignty in a Toxic World." *Cultural Anthropology* 33 (3): 415–43.

Lassiter, Luke Eric. 2005. *The Chicago Guide to Collaborative Ethnography.* Chicago: University of Chicago Press.

Latour, Bruno. 1991. *We Have Never Been Modern.* Cambridge, MA: Harvard University Press.

Lear, Jonathan. 2006. *Radical Hope: Ethics in the Face of Cultural Devastation.* Boston: Harvard University Press.

Leistle, Bernhard. 2014. "From the Alien to the Other: Steps Towards a Phenomenological Theory of Spirit Possession." *Anthropology of Consciousness* 25 (1): 53–90.

———. 2016. "Responsivity and (Some) Other Approaches to Alterity." *Anthropological Theory* 16 (1): 48–74.

Leshner, Alan. 1997. "Addiction Is a Brain Disease, and It Matters." *Science* 278 (5335): 45–47.

Levi-Strauss, Claude. 1963. "The Effectiveness of Symbols." In *Structural Anthropology*, translated by Claire Jacobson and Brooke Grundfest Schoepf, 186–205. Basic Books.

Lienhardt, Godfrey. 1961. *Divinity and Experience: The Religion of the Dinka.* Oxford: Oxford University Press.

Lock, Margaret, and Vinh-Kim Nguyen. 2010. *An Anthropology of Biomedicine.* Hoboken, NJ: Wiley.

Lovell, Anne, U. M. Read, and C. Lang. 2019. "Genealogies and the New Anthropologies of Global Mental Health." *Culture, Medicine and Psychiatry* 43 (4): 519–47.

Luedke, Tracy J., and Harry G. West, eds. 2006. *Borders and Healers: Brokering Therapeutic Resources in Southeast Africa.* Bloomington: Indiana University Press.

Luhrmann, Tanya Marie. 2012. *When God Talks Back: Understanding the American Evangelical Relationship with God.* New York: Alfred A. Knopf.

MacAndrew, Craig, and Robert Edgerton. 1969. *Drunken Comportment: A Social Explanation.* Chicago: Aldine Publishing Company.

Macintyre, Kate. 2011. "Alcohol Brewing and the African Tuberculosis Epidemic." *Medical Anthropology* 30 (2): 126–35.

Mahmood, Saba. 2004. *Politics of Piety: The Islamic Revival and the Feminist Subject.* Princeton NJ: Princeton University Press.

Mallaby, Sebastian. 2004. *The World's Banker: A Story of Failed States, Financial Crises, and the Wealth and Poverty of Nations.* New York: Penguin Press.

Marshall, Mac. 1979. *Weekend Warriors: Alcohol in a Micronesian Culture.* Palo Alto: Mayfield Publishing Co.

Marshall, Mac, Genevieve M. Ames, and Linda A. Bennett. 2001. "Anthropological Perspectives on Alcohol and Drugs at the Turn of the New Millennium." *Social Science & Medicine* 53 (2): 153–64.

Marshall, Ruth. 2016. "Destroying Arguments and Captivating Thoughts: Spiritual Warfare Prayer as Global Praxis." *Journal of Religious and Political Practice* 2 (1): 92–113.

Martinez, Priscilla, Irene Andia, Nneka Emenyonu, Judith A. Hahn, Edvard Hauff, Larry Pepper, and David R. Bangsberg. 2008. "Alcohol Use, Depressive Symptoms and the Receipt of Antiretroviral Therapy in Southwest Uganda." *AIDS and Behavior* 12 (4): 605–12.

Masquelier, Adeline. 2001. *Prayer Has Spoiled Everything: Possession, Power, and Identity in an Islamic Town of Niger*. Durham, NC: Duke University Press Books.

———. 2019. *Fada: Boredom and Belonging in Niger*. Chicago: University of Chicago Press.

Mattingly, Cheryl. 2010. *The Paradox of Hope: Journeys Through a Clinical Borderland*. Berkeley: University of California Press.

———. 2014. *Moral Laboratories: Family Peril and the Struggle for a Good Life*. Oakland: University of California Press.

———. 2018. "Ordinary Possibility, Transcendent Immanence, and Responsive Ethics: A Philosophical Anthropology of the Small Event." *HAU: Journal of Ethnographic Theory* 8 (1–2).

Mattingly, Cheryl, Rasmus Dyring, Maria Louw, and Thomas Schwarz Wentzer, eds. 2017. *Moral Engines: Exploring the Ethical Drives in Human Life*. New York: Berghahn Books.

Maxwell, David. 2005. "The Durawall of Faith: Pentecostal Spirituality in Neo-Liberal Zimbabwe." *Journal of Religion in Africa* 35 (1): 4–32.

Mbiti, John. 1970. *Concepts of God in Africa*. London: Society for Promoting Christian Knowledge.

Mbulaiteye, S. M., A. Ruberantwari, J. S. Nakiyingi, L. M. Carpenter, A. Kamali, and J. A. Whitworth. 2000. "Alcohol and HIV: A Study among Sexually Active Adults in Rural Southwest Uganda." *International Journal of Epidemiology* 29 (5): 911–15.

McCall, Michael. 2002. "Brewers, Woodfuel, and Donors: An Awkward Silence as the Fires Blaze." In *Alcohol in Africa: Mixing Business, Pleasure, and Politics*, edited by Deborah Fahy Bryceson, 93–114. Portsmouth, NH: Heinemann.

McCloud, Sean. 2015. *American Possessions: Fighting Demons in the Contemporary United States*. Oxford: Oxford University Press.

McGruder, Juli. 2004. "Madness in Zanzibar: An Exploration of Lived Experience." In *Schizophrenia, Culture and Subjectivity*, edited by Janis Jenkins and Robert Barrett, 255–81. Cambridge: Cambridge University Press.

McLellan, Thomas, and Anna Rose Childress. 1985. "Aversive Therapies for Substance Abuse: Do They Work?" *Journal of Substance Abuse Treatment* 2 (3): 187–91.

Meinert, Lotte. 2020. "Haunted Families After the War in Uganda: Doubt as Polyvalent Critique." *Ethnos* 85 (4): 595–611.

Melly, Caroline. 2017. *Bottleneck: Moving, Building, and Belonging in an African City*. Chicago: University of Chicago Press.

Meyer, Birgit. 1998. "'Make a Complete Break with the Past': Memory and Post-Colonial Modernity in Ghanaian Pentecostalist Discourse." *Journal of Religion in Africa* 28 (3): 316–49.

———. 1999. *Translating the Devil: Religion and Modernity among the Ewe in Ghana*. Trenton, NJ: Africa World Press.

Mittermaier, Amira. 2011. *Dreams That Matter: Egyptian Landscapes of the Imagination*. Berkeley: University of California Press.

———. 2012. "Dreams from Elsewhere: Muslim Subjectivities beyond the Trope of Self-Cultivation." *Journal of the Royal Anthropological Institute* 18 (2): 247–65.

Mkhwanazi, Nolwazi. 2016. "Medical Anthropology in Africa: The Trouble with a Single Story." *Medical Anthropology* 35 (2): 193–202.

Mol, Annemarie. 2003. *The Body Multiple: Ontology in Medical Practice*. Durham, NC: Duke University Press.

Moll, Yasmin. 2018. "Television Is Not Radio: Theologies of Mediation in the Egyptian Islamic Revival." *Cultural Anthropology* 33 (2): 233–65.

Moore, Erin. 2016. "Postures of Empowerment: Cultivating Aspirant Feminism in a Ugandan NGO." *Ethos* 44 (3): 375–96.

———. 2020. "What the Miniskirt Reveals: Sex Panics, Women's Rights, and Pulling Teeth in Urban Uganda." *Anthropological Quarterly* 93 (3): 321–50.

Mosko, Mark. 2010. "Partible Penitents: Dividual Personhood and Christian Practice in Melanesia and the West." *Journal of the Royal Anthropological Institute* 16 (2): 215–40.

Musinguzi, Geofrey, Denis Bwayo, Noah Kiwanuka, Sheila Coutinho, Aggrey Mukose, Joseph Kabanda, Lilian Sekabembe, and Fred Nuwaha. 2014. "Sexual Behavior among Persons Living with HIV in Uganda: Implications for Policy and Practice." *PLoS ONE* 9 (1): 1–10.

Mutibwa, Phares. 1992. *Uganda Since Independence: A Story of Unfulfilled Hopes*. London: Hurst.

Myhre, Knut Christian. 2019. "Tales of a Stitched Anus: Fictions, Analytics, and Personhood in Kilimanjaro, Tanzania." *Journal of the Royal Anthropological Institute* 25 (1): 9–28.

Nannyonga-Tamusuza, Sylvia Antonia. 2005. *Baakisimba: Gender in the Music and Dance of the Baganda People of Uganda*. London: Routledge.

Netherland, Julie, and Helena Hansen. 2016a. "The War on Drugs That Wasn't: Wasted Whiteness, 'Dirty Doctors,' and Race in Media Coverage of Prescription Opioid Misuse." *Culture, Medicine, and Psychiatry* 40 (4): 664–86.

———. 2016b. "White Opioids: Pharmaceutical Race and the War on Drugs That Wasn't." *BioSocieties* 12 (2): 217–38.

Nichter, Mark, and Gilbert Quintero. 2004. "Qualitative Research: Contributions to the Study of Drug Use, Drug Abuse, and Drug Use(r)-Related Interventions." *Substance Use & Misuse* 39 (10–12): 1907–69.

Obbo, Christine. 1996. "Healing, Cultural Fundamentalism, and Syncreticism in Buganda." *Africa* 66 (2): 183–201.

Obrist, Brigit, and Peter Van Euwijk. 2020. "Medical Anthropology in, of, for, and with Africa: Three Hotspots." *Medical Anthropology* 9 (8): 782–93.

Okiror, Ben. 2009. "From an Alcoholic to Academic Ace." *The New Vision*, April 10, 2009, sec. Archive. https://www.newvision.co.ug/news/1223026/alcoholic-academic-ace.

Okungu, Jerry. 2010. "How Many People Must Be Blinded, Killed by Gin?" *The New Vision*, May 20, 2010, sec. Columnists. http://www.newvision.co.ug/D/8/20/720164.

Olorunfemi, A. 1984. "The Liquor Traffic Dilemma in British West Africa: The Southern Nigerian Example, 1895–1918." *International Journal of African Historical Studies* 17 (2): 229–41.

O'Neill, Kevin Lewis. 2019. *Hunted: Predation and Pentecostalism in Guatemala*. Chicago: University of Chicago Press.

Ong, Aihwa, and Stephan Collier, eds. 2005. *Global Assemblages: Technology, Politics, and Ethics as Anthropological Problems*. Malden: Blackwell.

Orsi, Robert. 2018. *History and Presence*. Cambridge, MA: Harvard University Press.

Ortega, Ian. 2012. "Rehab Diary: Finally the End Arrives." *The Monitor*, August 19, 2012, sec. Life. http://www.monitor.co.ug/Magazines/Life/Finally-the-end-arrives/-/689856 /1481934/-/5u8a11z/-/index.html.

Osseo-Asare, Abena-Dove. 2014. *Bitter Roots: The Search for Healing Plants in Africa*. Chicago: University of Chicago Press.

Peterson, Derek. 2016. "A History of the Heritage Economy in Yoweri Museveni's Uganda." *Journal of East African Studies* 10 (4): 789–806.

Pierre, Jemima. 2012. *The Predicament of Blackness: Postcolonial Ghana and the Politics of Race*. Chicago: University of Chicago Press.

van de Port, Mattijs. 2011. *Ecstatic Encounters: Bahian Candomble and the Quest for the Really Real*. Amsterdam: Amsterdam University Press.

Povinelli, Elizabeth. 2011. *Economies of Abandonment: Social Belonging and Endurance in Late Liberalism*. Durham, NC: Duke University Press.

———. 2015. "Transgender Creeks and the Three Figures of Power in Late Liberalism." *Differences: A Journal of Feminist Cultural Studies* 26 (1): 168–87.

Pringle, Yolana. 2019. *Psychiatry and Decolonisation in Uganda*. London: Palgrave MacMillan.

Prussing, Erica. 2011. *White Man's Water: The Politics of Sobriety in a Native American Community*. Tucson: University of Arizona Press.

Pype, Katrien. 2011. "Confession Cum Deliverance: In/Dividuality of the Subject Among Kinshasa's Born-Again Christians." *Journal of Religion in Africa* 41: 280–310.

Qian, Frank, Temidayo Ogundiran, Ningqi Hou, Paul Ndom, Antony Gakwaya, Johashaphat Jombwe, Imran Morhason-Bello, et al. 2014. "Alcohol Consumption and Breast Cancer Risk among Women in Three Sub-Saharan African Countries." *PLoS ONE* 9 (9): 1–12.

Qu, Ray. 2022. "The Quest for a Good Life: Incense Seeing and the Porous and Dividual Hoping Person in North China." *American Anthropologist* 124 (2): 252–62.

Rabinow, Paul. 2003. *Anthropos Today: Reflections on Modern Equipment*. Princeton, NJ: Princeton University Press.

Raikhel, Eugene. 2016. *Governing Habits: Treating Alcoholism in the Post-Soviet Clinic*. Ithaca, NY: Cornell University Press.

Raikhel, Eugene, and William Garriott. 2013. *Addiction Trajectories*. Durham, NC: Duke University Press.

Ramberg, Lucinda. 2014. *Given to the Goddess: South Indian Devadasis and the Sexuality of Religion*. Durham, NC: Duke University Press.

Reid, Richard. 2017. *A History of Modern Uganda*. Cambridge: Cambridge University Press.

Rekdal, Ole Bjorn. 1999. "Cross-Cultural Healing in East African Ethnography." *Medical Anthropology Quarterly* 13 (4): 458–82.

Robbins, Joel. 2004. *Becoming Sinners: Christianity and Moral Torment in Papua New Guinea Society*. Berkeley: University of California Press.

———. 2013. "Beyond the Suffering Subject: Toward an Anthropology of the Good." *Journal of the Royal Anthropological Institute* 19: 447–62.

———. 2020. *Theology and the Anthropology of Christian Life*. Oxford: Oxford University Press.

Robbins, Joel, and Leanne Williams Green. 2017. "In What Does Failure Succeed? Conceptions of Sin and the Role of Human Moral Vulnerability in Pentecostal and Charismatic

Christianity." In *Straying from the Straight Path: How Senses of Failure Invigorate Lived Religion*, edited by D. Beeker and D. Kloos, 21–36. New York: Berghahn Books.

Roberts, Elizabeth. 2012. *God's Laboratory: Assisted Reproduction in the Andes*. Berkeley: University of California Press.

Roberts, Johnathan. 2010. "Michael Power and Guinness Masculinity in Africa." In *Beer in Africa: Drinking Spaces, States, and Selves*, edited by Steven van Van Wolputte and Mattia Fumanti, 29–52. Berlin: Lit Verlag.

Room, Robin. 1984. "Alcohol and Ethnography: A Case of Problem Deflation? [And Comments and Reply]." *Current Anthropology* 25 (2): 169–91.

Sanders, Todd. 2003. "Reconsidering Witchcraft: Postcolonial Africa and Analytic (Un)Certainties." *American Anthropologist* 105 (2): 338–52.

Scherz, China. 2010. "'You Aren't the First and You Won't Be the Last': Reflections on Moral Change in Contemporary Rural Ireland." *Anthropological Theory* 10 (3): 303–18.

———. 2013. "Let Us Make God Our Banker: Ethics, Temporality, and Agency in a Ugandan Charity Home." *American Ethnologist* 40 (4): 624–36.

———. 2014. *Having People, Having Heart: Charity, Sustainable Development, and Problems of Dependence in Central Uganda*. Chicago: University of Chicago Press.

———. 2018a. "Enduring the Awkward Embrace: Personhood and Ethical Work in a Ugandan Convent." *American Anthropologist* 120 (1): 102–12.

———. 2018b. "Stuck in the Clinic: Vernacular Healing and Medical Anthropology in Contemporary Sub-Saharan Africa." *Medical Anthropology Quarterly* 32 (4): 539–55.

Scherz, China, and George Mpanga. 2019. "His Mother Became Medicine: Ancestral Spirits, Drinking Problems and Maternal Care in Central Uganda." *Africa* 89 (1): 125–46.

Scherz, China, George Mpanga, and Sarah Namirembe. 2022. "Not You: Addiction, Relapse and Release in Uganda." *Culture, Medicine and Psychiatry*. 46 (1): 101–14.

Schoenbrun, David Lee. 1998. *A Green Place, A Good Place: Agrarian Change, Gender, and Social Identity in the Great Lakes Region to the 15th Century*. Portsmouth, NH: Heinemann.

Schonberg, Jeffery, and Philippe Bourgois. 2009. *Righteous Dopefiend*. Berkeley: University of California Press.

Schumaker, Lyn. 2001. *Africanizing Anthropology: Fieldwork, Networks, and the Making of Cultural Knowledge in Central Africa*. Durham, NC: Duke University Press.

Schwartz, Jeremy I., David Guwatudde, Rachel Nugent, and Charles Mondo Kiiza. 2014. "Looking at Non-Communicable Diseases in Uganda through a Local Lens: An Analysis Using Locally Derived Data." *Globalization and Health* 10: 77.

Schwarz Wentzer, Thomas. 2014. "'I Have Seen Konigsberg Burning': Philosophical Anthropology and the Responsiveness of Historical Experience." *Anthropological Theory* 14 (1): 27–48.

Segawa, Nakisanze. 2019. "Traditional Healers Don't Want Their Herbs Regulated, Citing Risk to Intellectual Property." *Global Press Journal*, 2019. https://globalpressjournal.com /africa/uganda/ugandan-bill-regulate-herbs-met-mistrust-traditional-healers.

Sharp, Lesley. 1994. *The Possessed and the Dispossessed*. Berkeley: University of California Press.

Simpson, Audra. 2014. *Mohawk Interruptus: Political Life Across the Borders of Settler States*. Durham, NC: Duke University Press.

Singer, Merrill. 1986. "Toward a Political-Economy of Alcoholism: The Missing Link in the Anthropology of Drinking." *Social Science & Medicine* 23 (2): 113–30.

Singer, Merrill, Freddie Valentin, Hans Baer, and Zhongke Jia. 1992. "Why Does Juan García Have a Drinking Problem? The Perspective of Critical Medical Anthropology." *Medical Anthropology* 14: 77–108.

Smith, J. W. 1982. "Treatment of Alcoholism in Aversion Conditioning Hospitals." In *Encyclopedic Handbook of Alcoholism*, edited by E. M. Pattison and E. Kaufman. New York: Gardner.

Spicer, P. 2001. "Culture and the Restoration of Self among Former American Indian Drinkers." *Social Science & Medicine (1982)* 53 (2): 227–40.

Ssebunnya, Joshua, Caroline Kituyi, Justine Nabanoba, Juliet Nakku, Arvin Bhana, and Fred Kigozi. 2020. "Social Acceptance of Alcohol Use in Uganda." *BMC Psychiatry* 20 (1): 1–7.

Ssekandi, I., A. Ssetaala, J. Mpendo, A. Nanvubya, L. Nielsen, and N. Kiwanuka. 2012. "Alcohol and Illicit Drug Use among Potential HIV Vaccine Efficacy Trial Volunteers along Lake Victoria, Uganda." *Retrovirology* 9 (Suppl+2): P219.

Ssenkaaba, Stephen. 2009. "Liver Diseases—Don't Wait for Signs, It May Be Too Late." *The New Vision*, July 19, 2009, sec. Health & Fitness.

Stevenson, Lisa. 2014. *Life Beside Itself: Imagining Care in the Canadian Arctic*. Oakland: University of California Press.

Stoller, Paul. 1989. *Fusion of the Worlds: An Ethnography of Possession Among the Songhay of Niger*. Chicago: University of Chicago Press.

Stonington, Scott. 2020. "Karma Masters: The Ethical Wound, Hauntological Choreography, and Complex Personhood in Thailand." *American Anthropologist* 122 (4): 759–70.

Strathern, Marilyn. 1988. *The Gender of the Gift: Problems with Women and Problems with Society in Melanesia*. Berkeley: University of California Press.

Street, Alice. 2014. *Biomedicine in an Unstable Place: Infrastructure and Personhood in a Papua New Guinean Hospital*. Durham, NC: Duke University Press.

Stroeken, Koen. 2010. *Moral Power: The Magic of Witchcraft*. New York: Berghahn Books.

Swahn, Monica H., Rachel Culbreth, Nazarius M. Tumwesigye, Volkan Topalli, Eric Wright, and Rogers Kasirye. 2018. "Problem Drinking, Alcohol-Related Violence, and Homelessness among Youth Living in the Slums of Kampala, Uganda." *International Journal of Environmental Research and Public Health* 15 (6): 1061.

Tallbear, Kim. 2017. "Beyond the Life/Not Life Binary: A Feminist-Indigenous Reading of Cryopreservation, Interspecies Thinking and the New Materialisms." In *Cryopolitics: Frozen Life in a Melting World*, edited by Joanna Radin and Emma Kowal, 179–202. Cambridge, MA: MIT Press.

Taylor, Christopher. 1992. *Milk, Honey, and Money: Changing Concepts of Rwandan Healing*. Washington, DC: Smithsonian Institution Press.

Thompson, E. P. 1967. "Time, Work-Discipline and Industrial Capitalism." *Past and Present* 38: 56–97.

Thornton, Robert. 2017. *Healing the Exposed Being: A South African Ngoma Tradition*. Johannesburg: Wits University Press.

Throop, Jason. 2018. "Being Open to the World." *HAU: Journal of Ethnographic Theory* 8 (1–2): 197–210.

Todd, Zoe. 2016. "An Indigenous Feminist's Take on the Ontological Turn: 'Ontology' Is Just Another Word for Colonialism." *Journal of Historical Sociology* 29 (1): 4–22.

Turner, Victor. 1967. *The Forest of Symbols: Aspects of Ndembu Ritual*. Ithaca, NY: Cornell University Press.

———. 1968. *The Drums of Affliction: A Study of Religious Processes among the Ndembu of Zambia*. Oxford: Oxford University Press with the International African Institute.

UBOS. 2014. *National Population and Housing Census 2014: Provisional Results*. Kampala: Uganda Bureau of Statistics.

Valverde, Mariana. 1998. *Diseases of the Will: Alcohol and the Dilemmas of Freedom*. Cambridge: Cambridge University Press.

Victor, Letha. 2019. "Those Who Go Underwater: Indignation, Sentiment, and Ethical Immanence in Northern Uganda." *Anthropological Theory* 19 (3): 385–411.

Victor, Letha, and Holly Porter. 2017. "Dirty Things: Spiritual Pollution and Life After the Lord's Resistance Army." *Journal of East African Studies* 11 (4): 590–608.

Vice. 2012. "Uganda's Moonshine Epidemic." https://www.youtube.com/watch?v=zL3UHF5SlEU.

Vorhölter, Julia. 2017. "Class-Based Chronicities of Suffering and Seeking Help: Comparing Addiction Treatment Programs in Uganda." *Culture, Medicine and Psychiatry* 41 (4): 564–89.

Wainaina, Binyavanga. 2005. "How to Write About Africa." *Granta*, 2005.

Waldenfels, Bernhard. 2011. *Phenomenology of the Alien*. Evanston, IL: Northwestern University Press.

Ward, C. 1980. "Spirit Possession and Mental Health: A Psycho-Anthropological Perspective." *Human Relations* 33 (3): 149–63.

Wasswa, Anatoli, and Henry Ford Miirima. 2006. *Unveiling Witchcraft*. Kisubi: Marianum Press.

Watters, Ethan. 2010. *Crazy like Us: The Globalization of the Western Mind*. New York: Free Press.

Watts, Vanessa. 2013. "Indigenous Place-Thought and Agency Amongst Humans and Non Humans (First Woman and Sky Woman Go On a European World Tour!)." *Decolonization: Indigeneity, Education, and Society* 2 (1): 20–34.

Werbner, Richard P. 2011. *Holy Hustlers, Schism, and Prophecy: Apostolic Reformation in Botswana*. Berkeley: University of California Press.

Whitmarsh, Ian, and Elizabeth Roberts. 2016. "Nonsecular Medical Anthropology." *Medical Anthropology* 35 (3): 203–8.

Whyte, Susan Reynolds. 1997. *Questioning Misfortune*. Cambridge: Cambridge University Press.

Willis, Justin. 2002. *Potent Brews : A Social History of Alcohol in East Africa, 1850–1999*. Athens: Ohio University Press.

———. 2007. "Clean Spirit: Distilling, Modernity and the Ugandan State, 1950–86." *Journal of East African Studies* 1: 79–92.

Wilson, Godfrey. 1942. *An Essay on the Economics of Detribalization in Northern Rhodesia (Part 2)*. Rhodes-Livingstone Paper No. 6. Livingstone, Northern Rhodesia: Rhodes-Livingstone Institute.

Wolff, Brent, Joanna Busza, Leonard Bufumbo, and Jimmy Whitworth. 2006. "Women Who Fall by the Roadside: Gender, Sexual Risk and Alcohol in Rural Uganda." *Addiction* 101 (9): 1277–84.

World Health Organization. 2004. "Global Status Report on Alcohol 2004." Geneva: World Health Organization.

———. 2013. "WHO Traditional Medicine Strategy: 2014–2023." Geneva: World Health Organization.

———. 2014. "Global Status Report on Alcohol and Health 2014." Geneva: World Health Organization.

Zablotska, Iryna B., Ronald H. Gray, Michael A. Koenig, David Serwadda, Fred Nalugoda, Godfrey Kigozi, Nelson Sewankambo, Tom Lutalo, Fred Wabwire Mangen, and Maria Wawer. 2009. "Alcohol Use, Intimate Partner Violence, Sexual Coercion and HIV among Women Aged 15–24 in Rakai, Uganda." *AIDS and Behavior* 13 (2): 225–33.

Zigon, Jarrett. 2007. "Moral Breakdown and the Ethical Demand: A Theoretical Framework for an Anthropology of Moralities." *Anthropological Theory* 7 (2): 131–50.

———. 2008. *Morality: An Anthropological Perspective*. Oxford: Berg Publishers.

———. 2011. *HIV Is God's Blessing: Rehabilitating Morality in Neoliberal Russia*. Berkeley: University of California Press.

———. 2018. *A War on People: Drug User Politics and a New Ethics of Community*. Berkeley: University of California Press.

———. 2021. "How Is It Between Us? Relational Ethics and Transcendence." *Journal of the Royal Anthropological Institute* 27 (2): 384–401.

Zoanni, Tyler. 2018. "The Possibilities of Failure: Personhood and Cognitive Disability in Urban Uganda." *The Cambridge Journal of Anthropology* 36 (1): 1–22.

———. 2019. "Appearances of Disability and Christianity in Uganda." *Cultural Anthropology* 34 (3): 444–70.

INDEX

141

Founded in 1893,
UNIVERSITY OF CALIFORNIA PRESS
publishes bold, progressive books and journals
on topics in the arts, humanities, social sciences,
and natural sciences—with a focus on social
justice issues—that inspire thought and action
among readers worldwide.

The UC PRESS FOUNDATION
raises funds to uphold the press's vital role
as an independent, nonprofit publisher, and
receives philanthropic support from a wide
range of individuals and institutions—and from
committed readers like you. To learn more, visit
ucpress.edu/supportus.

www.ingramcontent.com/pod-product-compliance
Lightning Source LLC
Chambersburg PA
CBHW030735280326
41926CB00086B/1634